Mickey
Thomas

Andy Strickland is Associate Editor of *Goal* magazine.

Mickey Thomas

Wild at Heart

Andy Strickland

B▦XTREE

First published in 1997 by Boxtree, an imprint of
Macmillan Publishers Ltd, 25 Eccleston Place, London, SW1W 9NF
and Basingstoke

Associated companies throughout the world

ISBN 0 7522 2481 6

9 8 7 6 5 4 3 2 1

A CIP catalogue record for this book is available
from the British Library

Typeset by SX Composing DTP, Rayleigh, Essex
Printed by Mackays of Chatham plc, Chatham, Kent

Picture Credits
Cover photographs: Colorsport
All other photographs: PA News

Preface

Football may or may not have come home in recent times, but in the mid 1970s, some people wouldn't give the English game house room. If the national team was a reflection of the state of the game generally, then English football was dying on its feet. In Europe, English clubs packed with Scots and Irish were ruling the roost, but England's failure to qualify for either the 1974 or 1978 World Cup Finals was a national disaster. A generation of football fans had been brought up with their earliest common memory being the 1966 World Cup Final and the scenes of red-shirted, Three Lions style joy that accompanied it. We expected England to win every single time they played. We'd been brought up sneaking downstairs and on to the end of the settee to watch the highlights from Wembley on Sportsnight – England always seemed to win 4-0.

The early 70s had put the disappointment of the Mexico World Cup behind it and spawned a group of players who would later revel in the collective title of 'The Mavericks'. These were hugely gifted players – like Peter Osgood, Alan Hudson, Stan Bowles and Tony Currie – who played and partied hard and were, almost without exception, overlooked when it came to sustained international honours. They played for big, glamorous clubs who never won the English league, clubs like Chelsea and Queens Park Rangers, and as they watched English football go down the pan they wasted no time in telling anyone who would listen that they could turn things around. No one was listening. They left these shores for America when the cheques were waved in front of their eyes and spent a few years living off their reputations, playing for club owners who wouldn't know an offside, let alone a decent player, if it kicked them in the face.

By the time managers and fans realised that these were the kind of players who might have matched the Johan Cruyffs and the Mario Kempeses, the mavericks were history. English football now demanded a more solid, dependable type of animal. While Bryan Robson, a magnificent competitor and captain admittedly, was being elevated to the level of national hero, players such as Hoddle, Brady and even Kevin Keegan were leaving for more appreciative audiences in Europe.

The maverick was no more. Now, instead we had wingers.

Mickey Thomas isn't as famous as Peter Osgood or Stan Bowles. Mickey Thomas may not even be as famous as his Arsenal namesake, who clinched the Title for the Highbury outfit at Anfield in 1991. If he'd been born six or seven years earlier he would be much in demand and he'd spend matchdays at Old Trafford welcoming guests to their executive boxes and signing programmes for light-engineering MDs from Salford. This, sadly, is the lot of the maverick in the late 90s. Mickey was probably Welsh football's first, and last, maverick. Except for the fact that he played for Manchester United – something none of his early 70s counterparts had done – and that he won 51 international caps. Oh, and that he preferred Colwyn Bay pier to Stringfellows.

By the time he joined his superstar pals at Old Trafford in 1978, he was almost a relic of a bygone era. A crucial and much loved relic – the fans demanded at least one player in the side who was an entertainer and, for all his tricky wing play and dazzling change of pace, Steve Coppell was never that – but a relic nonetheless.

No, they wanted footballing brilliance topped off with some sign of human frailty, and Mickey had that in buckets. He'd run his guts out for the team, try to nutmeg the same opponent time after time, and then we'd all read in the papers that his missus had thrown out his video and kicked in a plate glass door. Great stuff, he was one of us. Before Mickey became a United player, a natural and much needed replacement for the departed Gordon Hill, the team had made do with Ashley Grimes. Ashley Grimes? How many kids on the Stretford End could relate to a bloke called Ashley Grimes?

The club also saw Mickey as an early candidate in the time honoured search for the new George Best – who would have been King of the mavericks except he ruined it all by almost single-handedly winning the European Cup for United in 1968. It has been a long search now. Lee Sharpe, Ryan Giggs, even David Beckham, George is wheeled out once a year to pass judgement on the pretenders to his crown, but Mickey Thomas was always much closer to the free spirit that was George.

George Best didn't know what made him so brilliant. He couldn't explain his body swerve if you gave him all night. He honed it to perfection on the cinder training pitch at Old Trafford and it just came naturally. He may have worked like a dog on improving his heading and his weaker foot, but the talent was there when he got up in the morning and when he went to bed – whoever's it happened to be – that night.

Mickey was the only Welshman involved in the 1979 FA Cup final between Arsenal and Manchester United. He didn't have an outstanding match – he was too nervous for that – but he was the only player on the field that younger United fans still remember. Jimmy Greenhoff? Gordon McQueen? Don't think so.

Of course being arrested helps. Being attacked with a screwdriver while having sex in a car helps even more. There are celebrities who would pay tens of thousands of pounds for that sort of publicity. And, although he probably doesn't like to admit it, Mickey's more famous for his off-field adventures than for anything he ever achieved on it. Except that FA Cup goal against Arsenal, of course.

1: 'You'll Make A Great Carpet Fitter'

It was a beautiful July morning in Erddig Park, just a few miles outside Wrexham. The day was just beginning to warm up and the tall, straight pines echoed to the gentle sound of the pigeons high up in the trees. Then, almost imperceptibly at first, came the sounds of men running. Louder now and mixed with the occasional laugh, cough, and the unmistakable sound of footballers clearing throats and nostrils as only they know how. Their heads came into view first over the brow of the wide dirt track that cuts its way through the quiet country park; young, slim athletic, cropped haired men in a rag bag of t-shirts, baggy shorts and cotton drill tops, some bearing the wholly inappropriate legend, 'Wrexham Lager'. One youngster, no more than seventeen years old, set the pace, but behind him, running more relaxedly and determinedly than most around him was a stout balding red-faced man some twenty years his senior.

Mickey Thomas might not have still possessed the pace that had served him well through spells at Wrexham, Manchester

United, Everton, Brighton & Hove Albion, Stoke City, Chelsea, West Bromwich Albion, Derby County, Wichita Wings (USA), Shrewsbury Town, Leeds United, Stoke City again and back to Wrexham, but this was his twentieth pre-season and he wasn't about to lie down and become the butt of the trainees' jokes just yet. Professional footballers on the way up are notoriously no respecters of age but even with a court appearance for allegedly passing fake ten pound notes to some of his young colleagues hanging over him, Thomas had the air of a man determined to make the most of what might be his last season in professional football. Secretly he'd set himself a target of playing on until the age of forty.

From Mochdre, Colwyn Bay, to Manchester United and back again had been one of football's most controversial and improbable adventures, but more, much more was still to come.

When Michael Reginald Thomas was born on July 7 1954, there was little chance that he'd grow up unable to work magic with a football. The Thomas family from Colwyn Bay could already boast a football playing father and a brother who'd packed his bag and left a trial at West Ham United after just one day because he didn't like it in London. Young Michael, or 'Mickey', was soon knocking a ball, left footed, against the garden fence of the modest council house where the family lived, often until after midnight. His pocket money was blown immediately on football magazines, chewing gum cards, plastic balls which could be repaired over and over again with a hot knife, anything to do with the game – and Everton and his hero Alan Ball in particular.

'He was brilliant when he was at Everton,' said Mickey. 'Little tiger he was. Fantastic passer of the ball, I used to think about him all the time.' Ball was a bag of energy, but he also played with a passion and commitment that was an inspiration to young Mickey. His part in English football's finest hour had obviously marked him out as something special but his touch and quick football brain were exceptional and the scrawny young Welsh lad couldn't have picked a better role model.

Mickey's dad Reg also took Mickey to Goodison Park as often as he could where the pair would take up their position on the Gladwys Street end terrace. Mickey's school work inevitably suffered. So much so in fact that the local truancy and careers officer paid the Thomas household a visit. Her verdict? The young Mickey would make a great carpet fitter! Not a bad ambition for a lad from Mochdre in the 1950s perhaps, but Mickey was meant for greater things.

A small village a few miles outside the burgeoning North Wales holiday resort of Colwyn Bay, Mochdre sits in a dramatic valley, part of the gateway to Snowdonia, whose impressive peaks tower over the village and its unassuming collection of small shops, Mountain View pub, light industrial park and the neat council estate which still sits at its centre. The local playing field is lovingly tended – for cricket. In winter, this is a rugby village. The Thomas family broke with tradition when they played football, even in the more football friendly north of Wales with its Merseyside connections and its wealth of footballing talent. The country's most successful international stars – Neville Southall, Ian Rush, Gary Speed and Mark Hughes – all came from the North and yet many of Mickey's friends from the estate didn't have a chance to learn the game. Football was effectively banned at some schools and a young William Roach, Coronation Street's Ken Barlow, was one local youngster who was only ever to be seen playing rugby. Colwyn has had its share of celebrity residents: Timothy Dalton, Monty Python star Terry Jones, Norwich boss Mike Walker, and Flying Pickerts bass singer, Gareth Williams.

The residents of Mochdre could not have known that that nice Mrs Thomas' new baby would grow up to be their most famous, and infamous, son. In July 1954, they were more interested to hear that the local council had accepted a proposal that a new bus stop be erected on the estate, while the weekend preceding baby Michael's arrival, many of them had travelled into Colwyn Bay, having presumably walked some distance for a bus, to watch the new Danny Kaye film at the Odeon. *Knock On Wood* was enthusiastically billed as Kaye, 'at his Kaye-raziest, Kaye-lossal best,' and if they didn't fancy the rubber-faced, singing comedian they could always check out Issy Bonn, 'famous recording and Radio singing artiste' at the Arcadia Theatre. Indeed Welsh singing was currently the focus of much attention after English choirs had dominated at the Llangollen International Eisteddfod, taking four of the five major trophies.

Colwyn Bay's potential as a tourist attraction was just beginning to be realised and while the current fire brigade investigation into the safety of the North Wales coast's boarding houses would have been welcomed, a call in that week's *North Wales Pioneer* for greater use of Welsh national costume to help attract tourists, probably didn't get much support among the shoppers making their way through the stalls at Colwyn Bay's regular Saturday market.

The new football season was still some weeks off but two stories dominated the sports pages. Former Newport, West Bromwich Albion and Sheffield Wednesday player, Douglas Whitcomb was to take over as player/coach at Llandudno FC, but the biggest surprise of the week was the news that the Welsh League Division Three, Dyserth Area, had voted to stop its membership of the North Wales Inter Area Competition.

The Thomas family home is still there, painted white among its grey, cement-fronted neighbours, tucked away at the end of one of the many roads whose neat, hedge-fronted houses are now owned by their former council tenants. When the estate was built, the council evidently could not foresee a day when the majority of residents here would own a car, and today's drivers have to park on the kerb to save blocking the narrow roads.

Mickey's still there too, living back in his parent's old house behind a solid-looking front door beneath the only satellite dish in the street. A welcome refuge throughout a career, and a stormy marriage, that included countless disappearing acts, Mickey's modest home reflects his innate down-to-earth ordinariness as much as it does his post-football income. Ask his old drinking pals in the Marine Hotel in old Colwyn and they'll tell you. Mickey Thomas went from nowhere to the top and back down again, but he always kept his feet on the ground and remained unaffected by his fame.

Safe to say, he didn't invest his money wisely. A broken mar-

riage, maintenance for his two kids, Aaron and Jade, and a generous nature saw to that. When he left for America, and indoor
football with Wichita Wings, in the summer of 1986 the Colwyn
Bay minicab drivers were distraught. Mickey was one of their
best customers. He travelled everywhere by cab, it made drinking easier, and he never tipped less than five pounds a time.

The Marine was a convenient watering hole. Far enough out
of town to be a handy retreat, its three dark bars meant Mickey
could, if he felt like it, always find a quiet corner. It was also a
five-minute stroll from the beach where he would pound the
shoreline alone, early in the morning, to keep fit during the
summer, and, towards the end of his career, during an enforced
absence from the Wrexham training field. He claimed running
on sand helped give him the extra strength in his legs needed to
offset his slight frame and if the beach was a few minutes from
his favourite drinking hole – or one of them at least – then all
well and good.

Mickey moved on from this end of town when the noisy
Colwyn Bay expressway, a baffling, coast hugging motorway that
bypasses the town and was renowned as the most expensive
stretch of road ever built, was under construction. Nowadays the
unsuspecting visitor is more likely to be disturbed by the sound
of jet-skis skimming along from the old pier than by the sound
of Mickey's footsteps on wet sand along this part of the coast.

The Prom, and the pier in particular, were great meeting
places before the Expressway all but cut them off from the town.
When Mickey came home from Manchester he could take in
some live music here, maybe Madness, the Damned or

Desmond Dekker, all of whom trod the boards of the twice burnt down pier. Here, now, besides idle parking wardens and 'beach goods' huts, you can visit Dinosaur World, catch the free bus from the railway station to the Welsh Mountain zoo or simply stroll along the magnificent bay to another of Mickey's haunts, the Rhos Fynach pub in picturesque Rhos-on-Sea with its huddle of fishing boats, imposing Abbey Hotel and busy mini-cab office.

A plaque on the wall claims the Rhos Fynach used to be the home of Captain Henry Morgan who sailed the seven seas in the service of the English Queen Elizabeth I. It may or may not be true, but its owners now serve a decent pint of bitter while the regulars sing Welsh songs at increasing volume as closing time approaches. Ask them about Mickey Thomas and the bar staff pretend to be surprised he's a customer, 'Who? What – the footballer?'

But when Mickey fancies a drink outside Mochdre and the Mountain View, he can often be found here. It was the venue for an impromptu post-match party following his testimonial match against Wolverhampton Wanderers in July 1997 and on a fine evening it's a great place to breathe in the sea air and remind yourself why you always ran straight home to north Wales when the pressure got too much. Mickey did a lot of that.

People born and brought up by the sea find it an immensely calming and reassuring presence and Mickey was no different. That's why they always go back to it. The salt air, the sounds and the view all help of course, but the shore line and the water beyond represents a physical manifestation of the line between security and well-being on the one hand and uncertainty and danger beyond it. Mickey Thomas might not have realised it, but this is why he chose to run away to Colwyn Bay when the stresses and pressures of professional football got too much. If he'd been born in Bethnal Green, Moss Side or, heaven help him, Cardiff, he might never have walked out on Manchester United. But there was a lot of football to played before that fateful day.

2: The Racecourse Favourite

Wrexham Football Club was never likely to figure among the game's bigger names. Even allowing for the fact that North Wales has always proved a richer hunting ground for Welsh football scouts than has the south of the country, the club was originally formed by cricketers looking for some way to keep fit during the winter months. Those modest early ambitions were reflected in the club's achievements in the Third Division North before they made it into the new national Third Division in 1958, some eighty-six years after the club was formed.

Cardiff and Swansea had been fully integrated into the English league for nigh on forty years or more by then, despite Wrexham being the country's oldest club, and while the two southern 'giants' put all their efforts into hating each other, Wrexham looked up the road to Chester for their natural local rivals. The two clubs even kept their respective fans happy during the Second World War by playing a series of 'friendlies', although the inclusion in the Wrexham ranks of 'guest' players such as the mighty Stan Cullis and the legendary Stanley Matthews, gave the Racecourse team something of an advantage. Wrexham didn't even figure greatly in the shake-up of the Welsh Cup too often after winning it in 1931 when they thrashed Shrewsbury Town 7-0. After that, Chester and Swansea in particular, frequently proved to be their bogey teams.

By the time Mickey Thomas had got his first pair of football boots for Christmas, there were signs of better times ahead at Wrexham. They were still stuck in the Third Division North, but finished in eighth place the year he was born, and attracted their record home crowd of 34,445 three years later when they faced Manchester United in the fourth round of the FA Cup. United's 'Busby Babes' won 5-0, just a year before being wiped out in the Munich air crash, but the game seemed to kick-start an increased local interest in the club and that was reflected on the field when Wrexham finally lifted the Welsh Cup again in front of a 10,000 crowd consisting largely of shocked Swansea City fans at Cardiff's Ninian Park. Suddenly the locals started checking the results from the Racecourse as well as those of Everton and Manchester United – the area's more favoured clubs – and the following season they just made it into the new Third Division.

Life in the national league was far from easy and the achievements of the late 50s were soon forgotten as the club see-sawed between the third and fourth divisions. Disaster struck two months before Bobby Moore and England lifted the World Cup trophy at Wembley when Wrexham finished bottom of the Fourth Division and were forced to apply for re-election, which they did successfully. For a football-mad youngster showing great promise and approaching his twelfth birthday, it wasn't a position designed to encourage thoughts of a great future at the Racecourse.

Mickey was now turning out for both Clwyd & Conwy schools and North Wales schools representative sides, and scouts from Merseyside were to be seen jotting down his name in their notebooks as he tore down the left wing hitting crosses on to the heads of boys twice his size. Wrexham's John Neal also knew all about him. Physically, Mickey was still a long way short of most boys of his age, small, skinny and shy, but his speed and undoubted trickery on the ball kept him out of trouble on the pitch. On top of that, he already possessed a surprisingly powerful left foot.

Despite another Wrexham revival, which culminated in promotion back to the Third Division as runners-up behind Chesterfield in 1969-70 and saw Mickey join the club as an amateur, the youngster had his eye on Leeds United as the decade came to an end. Don Revie's Leeds team were grindingly, famously, irritatingly good. They engineered a new approach to English league football which coupled the boundless flair of players such as Peter Lorimer, Alan Clarke and Johnny Giles with the uncompromising, rough house tactics of Norman Hunter, Billy Bremner and big Jack Charlton. They'd also stolen a march on their rivals by introducing neat marketing touches such as numbered sock tags and tracksuits with the players' names on the back. The kids, in particular, found all this irresistible. Leeds meant business and they looked the part in their dramatic all white strip which echoed the mighty Real Madrid and showed every splash of mud, every drop of blood and bead of sweat, every ounce of effort.

Mickey felt he needed to have a crack at a footballing future beyond the confines of North Wales and the Third Division at Wrexham. Leeds, glamorous Leeds, looked a decent bet. Wrexham were already giving him some of the trappings of life at a professional club, but it was a slow progression to the full professional ranks and a first team spot looked a long way off with Wrexham's old guard ensuring the youngsters were made to wait. A sixteen-year-old had little chance of dislodging the likes of the legendary Arfon Griffiths MBE, even one as talented as young Mickey Thomas. Mickey wrote to Leeds requesting a trial, and waited for a reply.

And yet Wrexham were enjoying one of the club's more colourful periods now. Manager John Neal, who took control in September 1968, realised the club must move forward and establish a group of talented youngsters if Wrexham football club was to progress. As well as promotion in 1970, Wrexham had enjoyed not a little Cup success this season as well.

For a fourth-division team to face Liverpool and Manchester United in the FA and League Cups respectively in one season was a massive boost to both support and finances. It helped prove a point to disgruntled apprentices too. 54,096 spectators watched the Welshmen gallantly go down at Anfield 3-1 at the end of January. This, coming on the back of an equally hard fought 2-0 defeat at Old Trafford – George Best, Bobby Charlton and all – earlier in the season, helped persuade Mickey to pledge his future to Wrexham and also enabled John Neal to strengthen the squad.

The following season, 1970-71, some of Mickey's young club mates were given their chance. Suddenly Wrexham was an exciting club to play for and a creditable ninth place in the Third Division gave everyone hope that the best was still to come. Mickey, still not signed as a full professional, was sure his chance would come soon.

New Year's Day 1972 wasn't the most auspicious of debuts for a seventeen-year-old Welsh lad from Mochdre. For a start, Mickey never got off the substitutes bench at Dean Court where Wrexham were comprehensively stuffed 4-0 by Bournemouth. While any player wearing the number 12 shirt might have expected to figure in such circumstances, Mickey was at least spared the ignominy of a debut defeat. It was also the last time that season that he'd be left on the bench.

John Neal decided now was the right time to introduce the frail-looking, pacy, wide midfielder. A week after the Bournemouth rout, Mickey took a deep breath and trotted out wearing the number six shirt to the stirring strains of 'Men of Harlech' beneath a typically grey winter's afternoon at the Racecourse Ground. As the PA announcer ran through the line-up of the visitors, Blackburn Rovers, Mickey's family sat in the stand, proud as could be. Nobody could have predicted that he'd play his last league game here more than twenty years later.

Mickey made nineteen league appearances that first season, donning the famous red number eleven shirt when the mighty Arfon Griffiths succumbed to a nagging injury in February. His shirt was on loan, he assured the cocky youngster. Mickey scored three goals, against Bolton Wanderers, Mansfield Town and, most satisfyingly, in a 2-0 defeat of Swansea City.

But it was his performances in the Welsh Cup which really caught the eye as Wrexham swept past Oswestry Town, Aberystwyth, Newport County and the much fancied Cardiff City. Mickey wasn't fully fit for the first leg of the Final, played at the Racecourse Ground, but the 2-1 lead they took south to Ninian Park proved decisive and they ran out surprise 3-2 winners on aggregate, meaning Mickey would get his first taste of European football and the Cup Winners' Cup at the Racecourse next season.

The 1972-73 campaign kicked off with an away win at Southend and Mickey soon established himself with a regular spot which meant he would figure in the first European Cup Winners' Cup tie, away to FC Zurich of Switzerland. A full house of 20,000 watched the Welshmen earn a well deserved 1-1 draw and the town was buzzing when the Swiss arrived for the second leg and Wrexham's first ever European home match.

Led by the very experienced Mel Sutton, whom the crowd had forgiven for his Cardiff past after he put in a string of man of the match winning performances, Wrexham were soon all over their shell-shocked visitors like a rash. But the finishing didn't match the neat approach play and it was the Swiss who got their noses in front soon after the restart with a great diving header from Martinelli.

Wrexham rolled up their sleeves and came again and it was that man Mickey Thomas who eventually sent in a measured cross from the touchline which was met by Billy Ashcroft's powerful header. All square now and the Swiss were shaking in their boots. The 18,000 strong crowd roared their approval and Mickey was loving every minute of it. He held his head in his hands when a typically fierce drive rattled the Swiss crossbar, but Welsh nerves were finally settled when another cross from the left found that old European campaigner, Mel Sutton, who made no mistake and sent the ball crashing past the despairing Karl Grob in the Zurich goal. The Racecourse Ground had never seen anything like it and the roar could probably be heard back in Mochdre. Now, at last, Robins fans could hold their heads high whenever Cardiff fans began to list their club's own European exploits. It was an historic night in Wrexham and Mickey had more than played his part. He was just eighteen years old.

One month later, the Racecourse Ground was heaving once more as the Yugoslavs of Hajduk Split arrived for the Second Round first leg of the same competition. Could they do it again? It was harder playing the first leg at home. John Neal knew his team must take a goal, preferably two, advantage to Yugoslavia if they were stand any chance of progressing further. The players went through their usual pre-match routine as the crowds poured off the special trains laid-on to bring the masses in from Buckley, Pen-y-Ffordd, Yr Hob, Caergwerle, Cefn-y-bedd and Gwersyllt.

That night, Mickey and his team mates were simply brilliant. They put three goals past the Split keeper, two for Brian Tinnion, but the Yugoslavs scored a priceless 'away' goal that would count double in the event of an aggregate draw. 3-1 then, more European glory. Two days later Wrexham lost 4-0 away at Tranmere!

The one result John Neal's men didn't want in Yugoslavia was a 2-0 defeat to go out on the away goal rule. It happened, and the club's first season in Europe ended after four unforgettable nights. The small band of travelling Robins fans blamed the referee and the intimidating home crowd but it wouldn't be their last campaign on foreign soil and the team had done them proud.

The remainder of the 72-73 season was a bit of a letdown after those early heroics. Mickey had picked up an injury and was in and out of the team for the rest of the year before missing two months between late January and March when he returned briefly as a substitute and made only a handful of appearances for the remainder of the campaign. He had scored his first FA Cup goal in the 5-0 mauling of Darlington after the First Round tie went to a replay, but it was to be his only successful strike of a season in which he made twenty-three league appearances and the club finished a modest twelfth in Division Three.

The following season Mickey was to learn something of what it meant to be a footballing legend. Not for himself, he was still only nineteen, but Arfon Griffiths was back with a bang and he wanted his old number eleven shirt back. Mickey had kept hold of it, and scored, in the club's opening league fixture at home to Walsall but Arfon usually got what he wanted and he didn't fancy the number six shirt thanks all the same. He got the number eleven back, and Mickey sat frustrated, his appearances in the first team usually corresponding to injuries to the man who would eventually manage the club himself just four years later.

Arfon was a Wrexham man born and bred. He'd made his professional debut when Mickey Thomas was just three years old and won the Welsh Youth Cup with Wrexham in 1959, before being whisked off to the bright lights of London and Arsenal a season later. Like Mickey Thomas at Manchester United years later, Arfon's move perhaps came too early and he never settled at Highbury. He jumped at the chance to return to the Racecourse Ground just six months later for around half the £15,500 fee the Highbury outfit had paid for him originally. The Wrexham directors congratulated themselves on a good bit of business, but Griffiths' influence on the Welsh club would be massive.

Arfon set a club record 592 league appearances between 1959 and 1979 and became assistant manager to John Neal in the mid 70s before taking over in 1977 and steering the club to promotion to the Second Division for the very first time a year later. He left in 1981 on a matter of principle after a disagreement with the directors, but still lives and runs a business in Wrexham though he stays away from the club he helped shape over twenty-two years. His MBE was awarded in 1976 for services to Welsh football. He wasn't the sort of man to give Mickey Thomas his number eleven shirt without a fight, back in the early 70s, particularly as he'd finally received a long overdue Welsh call up in 1971 for the game at Swansea against Czechoslovakia. For a player from the Third Division it was recognition of a great forward talent. He was to become Wrexham's first regular Welsh international since Tommy Bamford, forty years before, and won seventeen caps between 1971 and 1977.

He couldn't have realised that the scrawny little kid with long hair who was waiting in the wings would win exactly three times as many Welsh caps and become as famous as him over the next twenty years – albeit for largely different reasons.

With an extra promotion spot up for grabs for the first time in the 1973-74 season, Wrexham set about the new campaign with some vigour, winning their first three matches and rallying again in the crucial pre-Christmas period with five wins on the trot. Mickey, in and out of the side once more, picked up another injury that was to keep him out of the picture for two months as Wrexham embarked on a fantastic FA Cup run leading to Turf Moor and Burnley in the quarter-finals. Mickey watched from the substitute's bench as his team mates lost 1-0, but their league form looked sure to put them in with a good chance of promotion. They needed it following an embarrassing Welsh Cup semi-final defeat at the hands of Stourbridge.

Wrexham finished the season in a frustrating fourth place and Mickey made just fourteen league appearances. He wasn't achieving the breakthrough he'd hoped for, but people had noticed him. Two goals against Plymouth had helped, but the Wrexham fans already looked forward to his darting runs and his thunderous left foot shots. He may have been impatient, but the fans agreed, here was one for the future.

The 1974-75 season once again saw Wrexham save their best for the Welsh Cup. A victory over Cardiff was always sweet, but when it was the Cup Final and it meant European football next year, it was all the more satisfying. Wrexham won both legs, lifting the trophy in Cardiff thanks to a 5-2 aggregate victory.

Mickey became the club's regular number six – that man Griffiths made forty league appearances – but once again injury restricted his chances though he still totalled twenty-nine league appearances. The club couldn't sustain the previous season's promotion push and slipped to a poor thirteenth spot come the end of April.

1975-76 was to be Wrexham's greatest season in European competition. The Welsh Cup win had seen them paired with Swedish Cup winners, Djurgardens IF, in September and while Mickey missed the game, the modest crowd of 9,009 watched as the Robins pulled a 2-1 win out of the hat thanks to goals from Arfon Griffiths and Gareth Davies. It hadn't been a convincing performance and the locals didn't hold out too much hope of a famous victory in Sweden. They weren't wrong. The Swedes were in the driving seat having scored an away goal themselves and when they went 1-0 up it didn't look good for the Welshmen. But the Swedes seemed to be content with an away goals victory and allowed Wrexham back into the match. Graham Whittle pulled one back and Wrexham were through to the next round.

Here they were paired with the impossibly named Stal Rzeszow of Poland and once again the Wrexham boys, including Mickey Thomas this time, did the business and won a difficult home leg 2-0. Only 9,613 paid to watch, but in an effort to drum up more away support, the club's directors tried a free away travel scheme for the league game at Halifax. It worked and the Robins won the game. Watching them play away, in England, could be fun.

Bonfire night saw Mickey blinking through red flare smoke in a packed, tight little ground somewhere in Poland, no one seemed quite sure where they were, but they were all agreed they couldn't get out of there quick enough. It was an intimidating atmosphere that had done for many British clubs in the past, but the Welsh nerve held firm and a hard-fought 1-1 draw meant the club were through to the quarter-finals of the Cup Winners' Cup. Back home, as they listened on transistor radios along Mold Road, Cup fever finally broke. Wrexham had become the first Third Division side to reach the quarter-finals.

The quarter-final draw meant one of the big boys of European competition coming to town. Talk in the pubs and clubs was of one of the big Italian clubs gracing the Racecourse Ground but nobody was too disappointed when the mighty Anderlecht of Belgium came out of the hat. RSC Anderlecht, to give them their full name, were no strangers to European finals. The draw sent Wrexham, and 2,000 fans, across the water to Belgium for the first leg and once again, the English, and to some extent the Welsh, press wrote off Wrexham before a ball was kicked.

The Belgians, and their 33,000 supporters, were finding John Neal's men more of a handful than they'd been led to believe and the Welshmen could have taken the lead early on when steely Mel Sutton nearly took the keeper's head off with a rocket of a shot. But it was the Belgians who took the lead after ten minutes when Van Binst beat Brian Lloyd in the Wrexham goal and the trumpets and bugles filled the night air.

Wrexham had their chances. Stuart Lee left his team mates open mouthed when he missed the target from ten yards out then watched a similar effort well saved. The Belgians were packed full of classy internationals – Rensenbrink, Van der Elst, Haan – but despite showing their skills they were finding the Wrexham defence difficult to break down.

As the game wore on and the Wrexham players realised they weren't going to be swamped, they became more adventurous themselves and asked questions of the Belgian defence. The brass band turned to whistles, demanding referee Marjan Rau blow for time. When he did, the relief in the Belgian camp was tangible. With the home leg to come John Neal and his team knew they'd scored a psychological victory at the very least, but they'd done more than that, they'd struck a blow for Welsh football.

Mickey had been nursing an injury after picking up a knock at Crystal Palace a fortnight earlier and though he made it through the game in Belgium and the home win against Hereford four days before the second leg, John Neal wouldn't risk him in the return leg against Anderlecht. It was a bitter disappointment, compounded by the fact that despite more heroics, and taking the lead through a Stuart Lee strike, Wrexham eventually went out 2-1 on aggregate after a Belgian equaliser flew in off the post.

Mickey smiled bravely as, all around him in the stand, supporters reckoned things would have been different if only he'd been fit enough to play and asked when he'd be back in the side to chase promotion. He didn't dare admit, even to himself, that he might not play again that season. He didn't. Anderlecht proved to be worthy Cup Winners' Cup winners, going on to beat West Ham in the final.

When Wrexham beat Sheffield Wednesday and Chester a month later, revenge for being knocked out of the Welsh Cup by their old rivals in February, there was talk of promotion along Mold Road. But one win in the last four games saw them finish in a slightly disappointing, though creditable, sixth place.

John Neal's team now looked to be ready for the big push towards Division Two. Neal was desperate for success, he knew his team was ready, and the early signs for the new season were good. Wrexham won four on the trot in October and Billy Ashcroft and Graham Whittle were scoring goals for fun. Mickey was rewarded with his first Welsh cap, against West Germany in Cardiff and alongside him was Arfon Griffiths. Wrexham fans were ecstatic. They had two players in the same Welsh team, playing at Ninian Park! Only the 0-2 defeat ruined the Wrexham party. Back in the league, they went to Chesterfield and beat them 6-0, put four past Chester at the Racecourse and another six past Port Vale. They'd also accounted for First Division Tottenham in the League Cup, beating them 3-2 at White Hart Lane. Mickey, always one for the big games, scored twice past mighty Pat Jennings. It was easily Wrexham's, and Mickey's, most consistent season. He missed just one league game, a home win against Walsall, and when the team completed three wins in a row by beating Peterborough United at the end of April, the bunting was on order, the champagne in the fridge, and the players were allowing themselves to think the job was all but finished.

Needless to say, Wrexham failed to win even one of their remaining five matches, including the last home match against champions elect, Mansfield, in front of a fantastic crowd of 20,754. Mickey had played forty-five league matches scoring six times. Ashcroft and Whittle had notched forty-eight league goals between them but still it wasn't enough. To make matters worse, they'd also been knocked out of the FA Cup by Cardiff. Fifth place was not what the doctor ordered and the Wrexham fans were devastated. This was the kind of disappointment that bigger clubs than theirs had found impossible to come to terms with in the past and it all proved too much for John Neal. He left in the summer for the manager's seat at Middlesbrough and the Wrexham board, fearful of the team breaking up, wasted no time in appointing Arfon Griffiths as his successor. Mickey's season did end on a high note however. He found himself sitting on the bench at Wembley on May 31, beneath the Royal Box, as his Welsh team mates sneaked a 1-0 win over England.

John Neal made a quick return to the Racecourse in the new season, to take the free-scoring Billy Ashcroft with him, but that enabled Griffiths to add to his squad. He brought in Hereford's Dixie McNeil as a replacement number nine and was rewarded with twenty-three goals including his first on his debut against Swindon.

When keeper Dai Davies arrived from Everton and immediately displaced club favourite, Barry Lloyd, and his successor, Eddie Niedzwiecki, eyebrows were raised, but a run of twenty league matches with just one defeat proved the wily old campaigner knew what he was doing. He even managed to make fifteen appearances himself, just to make sure Mickey Thomas couldn't claim the number eleven shirt as his own.

Thomas and his team mates knew they owed a huge debt to John Neal, but they were too busy enjoying the club's greatest ever season to give him too much thought. They clinched promotion with a 7-1 demolition of Rotherham United in April and then, despite a wobble, took the Championship with a 0-0 home draw in front of over 23,000 fans on May 1. Liverpool also travelled to the Racecourse in the League Cup and spoiled the home team's party by winning 3-1 in front of 25,641 spectators.

Wrexham fans still remember that May and that team, and so they should. While the Championship was won emphatically, the club also made its first foray into the latter stages of the FA Cup by beating Newcastle United in a thrilling replay on the way to the quarter-finals and a home draw against Arsenal. Dixie McNeil scored eleven goals in nine FA Cup ties, an admirable replacement for Billy Ashcroft who watched his old mates with envy from the North East. And if all this wasn't enough, Wrexham proved unstoppable in the Welsh Cup too. They saw off Chester and Cardiff and beat Bangor over two legs in the Final to ensure European football again the following season. Once again, Mickey had proved the model of consistency missing just three league games and playing nineteen cup matches. It was rumoured he might be the next player set for a big move.

But for now, aged twenty-four, Mickey was keen to enjoy his first pre-season as a champion and his name was still on the team sheet when Arfon Griffiths sent out his first Division Two team to face Brighton on the opening day of the new season. Mickey relished the challenge of tormenting new defences and was soon hitting the best goal-scoring run of his career.

There was to be no European glory this time around. Drawn away in the first leg of the Cup Winners' Cup against Yugoslavian side, NK Rijeka, Mickey couldn't unlock a determined and uncompromising defence. The home side recorded a comfortable 3-0 victory and looked odds-on favourites to complete the job in Wales two weeks later. For the second leg, Arfon Griffiths decided his experience would be vital and he named himself in the team as substitute. Dixie McNeil got the Robins off to a great start and when Les Cartwright added a second, the home crowd sensed another memorable European night might be on the cards. But sadly it wasn't to be and Mickey and his team consoled themselves with the thought that consolidation amongst higher company in the league was more important than chasing unrealistic European dreams.

Wrexham were unbeaten in their first six games and Mickey had notched his usual season's haul of six goals by the end of November. Having grabbed an equaliser at Filbert Street to thwart Leicester City on November 22, Mickey was at last handed the red number eleven for keeps. Only now, it was a Manchester United first team jersey and he'd played his last game for Wrexham – for the time being at least.

It was a nervous former FC Shalke player, Wayne Cegielski, who ran out of the Racecourse tunnel wearing Mickey Thomas' old shirt for the home game against Millwall just three days later. The home fans were devastated. Losing a footballing hero to another team without a proper chance to say goodbye, on home soil, is always traumatic. The fans felt cheated, their emotions never given free rein. They needed to sing Mickey's name one more time, to cheer him off the pitch and wish him well. But while his old team mates cantered to a welcome 3-0 victory, Mickey was 250 miles away at Stamford Bridge helping his new club beat Chelsea 1-0.

3: The Bionic Brat

With the swinging sixties coming to an end and a young Mickey Thomas on the verge of a footballing career, there was only one club in Britain that inspired awe in their opponents and opposition fans alike. Manchester United were simply magnificent. With the giant European Cup finally resting in the Old Trafford trophy room and an unbelievable forward line of Best, Law and Charlton drawing huge crowds wherever they went, they were the undisputed superstars of British, if not world, club football.

The people of North Wales knew all about United. Many of them supported Matt Busby's team and those who didn't, even Everton fans, had to admit they were head and shoulders above the rest.

The club itself had a huge, Manchester-based support, but it didn't stop there. United boasted sixty-seven supporters club branches in Britain alone and the Torbay Reds would leave home at 5.30am on match days. Three times a season a plane load of fans would arrive from Malta and no fewer than fifty luxury coaches left Old Trafford for each away game.

If Mickey had allowed himself to dream that he might at least have a chance of a trial with the emerging Leeds United, or one day play for Everton, he didn't dare countenance the possibility that he would ever pull on the famous red jersey of United.

And yet it was a very different Manchester United that he joined for the game at Chelsea in November 1978. The club had just come out of its worst spell in living memory, having been relegated into the Second Division in 1974, but they'd proved far too good for the lower league and were immediately returned as Champions a year later. In 1977 they won the FA Cup, overcoming English football's new masters, Liverpool, and looked to be back on track with an exciting young team blended together brilliantly by their wily Scottish manager, Tommy Docherty.

Gordon Hill and Steve Coppell were arguably the best two wingers in the country and while Mickey Thomas was plying his trade at Chesterfield, Lincoln, Colchester and Rotherham in the 1977-78 season, the two United stars were to be found turning it on at Arsenal, Newcastle, Liverpool and Leeds. They weren't exactly looking over their shoulders, expecting a challenge from a little Welsh lad from Mochdre. But then they weren't expecting Tommy Docherty to leave the club either.

Following revelations that 'The Doc' was having an affair with the wife of the club's physio, Laurie Brown, he was forced to quit and in his place came the quiet, thoughtful Dave Sexton. The contrast between the two managers couldn't have been more striking. Docherty loved the limelight, the fans, the adulation and prestige that came with the United job. Sexton, on the other hand, had trouble making himself heard in training if the players were chatting. Both men had managed Chelsea, but that was where the comparisons ended.

Changes were inevitable. Sexton's first season in charge was a disappointment. United were knocked out of the Cup competitions, Europe included, in the early stages, and tenth place in the league still wasn't good enough. To make matters worse, Gordon Hill left to team up once more with Tommy Docherty at Derby County. Sexton needed a left-sided midfielder, if not an out and out winger and he recalled watching a young Welshman torment West Germany's vastly experienced right-back, Bertie Vogts, on his debut at Cardiff eighteen months previously. Mickey Thomas was as good as on his way to Old Trafford.

It took six months of scouting and negotiation, but United finally persuaded the Wrexham board to accept £300,000 and Mickey, incredibly, was a Manchester United player. And not a very comfortable one at that. As he was driven to the club's famous Cliff training ground to meet Joe Jordan, Gordon McQueen, Lou Macari, the Greenhoff Brothers, Jimmy and Brian, and Steve Coppell, Mickey struggled to keep his breakfast down. He'd felt safe, part of the furniture, a star at Wrexham, but now he was having trouble convincing himself that he was ready for this new challenge. He'd give anything right now to be on the beach at Colwyn Bay.

The big Scots, Joe Jordan and Gordon McQueen, were relative new boys at Old Trafford themselves and they tried their best to calm Mickey's nerves. Sexton's imported players needed to stick together and they broke the ice by reminding Mickey they'd already beaten him on two occasions playing for Scotland. Mickey assured them he'd make up for it in the five-a-sides. But even here he felt isolated.

'It's a bit of a nuisance being Welsh sometimes,' he confided. 'We have international five-a-sides at Old Trafford and the other countries are well represented. But I have to play in the All-Star team. I might tell the lads that I do the work of two men on the field, but even I can't be a one-man five-a-side team!'

Mickey was soon christened 'The Bionic Brat' by Gordon McQueen, but he needn't have felt so insecure. After debuting at Stamford Bridge on November 25 he would miss only one league match during the remainder of the season. Football is full of strange coincidences and so it was that the Racecourse had to wait just four days to finally say gooodbye to its famous son. Mickey was swept through the car park and into the changing rooms when Wales faced Turkey, and won, 1-0. There was no Arfon in the team now, but still two Wrexham players took the pitch that night. Mickey's great mate Joey Jones had arrived from Liverpool and Dai Davies acknowledged the cheers of his regular fans as he took his place in goal. For ninety minutes it was like Mickey Thomas had never been away.

Back at United, Mickey worked tirelessly alongside Lou Macari, complementing Steve Coppell who continued to raid down United's right flank and supplying the crosses for Jordan and Greenhoff. Sexton had Mickey working hard on improving the quality of his crosses in training and he accepted that he was being asked to play a slightly different role.

'It's different to the one I had at Wrexham. I used to play central-midfield there and I wouldn't mind going back to that position. I'm more of an extra midfield man, really. I don't attack that much – I tend to spend most of my time dropping back to help out. But I'm not a very good passer of the ball.'

In December, Mickey made his home debut in an impressive 2-0 victory against Tottenham. Striker Andy Ritchie got back into the side and provided Mickey with another fruitful target and after the Spurs game he admitted that the nerves were gnawing away at his stomach.

'I didn't sleep for three days before I made my debut. I tend to get very nervous before games in any case and that one had me particularly worried. I stood behind the goal the day before the match trying to imagine what the atmosphere would be like. On the day it was unbelievable.

'When the fans chanted my name I was almost too embarrassed to wave. They were very good to me though. When I'd been playing well at Wrexham and thinking I might get a transfer, I used to think about the clubs that might want to buy me. I thought about United on one occasion and then said to myself, 'Don't be silly, you're not good enough for them'.

'After I agreed to sign, Wrexham wanted me to play one more game for them, at Leicester. That was a bit nerve-wracking for me because I was worried that I might get injured and the deal would be off. But luckily I came through okay, we drew 1-1 and I finished on a high note by scoring our goal.'

When Leeds United came to Old Trafford in March, Mickey realised one remaining ambition. Manchester United completed the double over their Yorkshire rivals and Mickey grabbed his first league goal for the club in a thrilling 4-1 win.

The FA Cup would prove an epic campaign with replays against Tottenham in the quarter-finals and Liverpool in the semis before the amazing final itself saw Arsenal grab an impossibly late winner. Mickey played his part to the full and ended the season with a losers medal and some unbelievable memories from his first season in the top-flight.

He'd also taken to drinking. United players were given the freedom of Manchester in the late 70s. Clubs, discos, restaurants – they all fell over themselves to invite the players into VIP areas. It was good for business and the owner's ego and the players weren't about to complain. The more 'sensible' United stars made use of a local showbusiness guest house that was the habitual home of comedians, dancers and strippers, passing through town as they played the clubs. 'The Biz' as it was known, was run by Thin Lizzy star Phil Lynott's mum Phyllis. The Biz was also frequented by snooker star Alex Higgins and whenever Thin Lizzy were in town, Phil would take in a match at his beloved United and then invite the players back to mum's for a bender. Footballers and musicians had long enjoyed a unique relationship. For the players, it was a relief to meet people more internationally famous than them, while the musicians couldn't believe that the young men entrusted with the job of playing for the clubs they'd supported all their lives were so keen to seek out their company. Both sides were used to big money, fame and the trappings and pressures that came with it and would swap stories long into the night. Lynott had even recorded a song about

George Best, 'For Those Who Love To Live', and The Biz was somewhere the players could relax away from the public glare.

Contrary to popular opinion, Mickey Thomas had never been a big drinker at Wrexham. The same culture just didn't exist among the Racecourse staff and while he enjoyed the occasional pint, it was only after joining Manchester United that Mickey found there were advantages to taking the 'occasional glass'. It settled the nerves for one thing and helped blot out the continuous gawping stares from strangers that all United players had to come to terms with. You couldn't take a dump without someone slipping an autograph book under the lavatory door. It was that bad.

'The pressure really got to me,' says Mickey. 'It was then that I started drinking a lot. I'd go out and hit the booze until the early hours. It got to the stage where I had to get pissed before I played or I couldn't handle it. In fact, I played better with a drink inside me as I felt more relaxed.'

Mickey had become accustomed to driving back to North Wales to escape the pressures whenever he could and he had been dating a local girl, Debbie Dean, for some time. Debbie's claim to fame was a fifth place in a recent Miss Wales contest. She was a link with home that the insecure Mickey needed. She was also a part of his life that he could claim as his own and he kept their relationship a secret, even from his team mates.

It was therefore understandable that the United players, assembling for training at the Cliff one summer's morning, professed themselves 'amazed' at news that their influential mid-fielder was married. Mickey and Debbie had slipped away during preparations for the new season's opening match away to Southampton (a 1-1 draw) for a hush-hush registry office ceremony which was kept a secret, even from the couple's families, until the last minute. The subterfuge even extended to not ordering a celebration cake in case friends found out, and while it kept the prying eye of the press away from the big day, it was an inauspicious start for a marriage that was to directly affect the youngster's career and keep the tabloid press in stories for years to come.

Dave Sexton survived at the United helm, largely thanks to the FA Cup run, and now there was a new season to be played. Mickey, watched uncomfortably by his new bride, played his part in an impressive start that saw United lose just once in their first nine games, including a goal for Mickey at Villa Park as United won 3-0. The team was strengthened by the addition of former Chelsea captain Ray 'Butch' Wilkins who cost the club almost three times Mickey's fee at £825,000. Wilkins was brilliant, directing play, spraying passes wide to Mickey and Steve Coppell and setting attack after attack in motion. He was in no doubt as to the importance of Mickey Thomas, but he found his new team mate's secret marriage unfathomable.

'Mickey is a tireless worker who never seems to run out of energy,' he said. 'He rarely strays from the left and I've lost count of the number of times I've seen him win the ball just outside his own penalty area. Mickey surprised us all by getting married recently. Apparently he's been engaged for some time and the other lads kept ribbing him about this, saying it was time he took the plunge.

'When we were down to play Arsenal we started to joke about this and he turned round and said: "How do you know I'm not already married?" We laughed it off, and to our amazement, read in the papers the next day that he was married the week before! Mickey said he didn't want any fuss.'

Mickey may have been feeling a touch insecure. A story did the rounds that Dave Sexton was lining up a swap deal with Everton's Dave Thomas and when Mickey heard the news he was shocked. Sexton wasted no time. As soon as he heard the rumour he rushed round to the player's house and told him he had no intention of selling him, or exchanging him, for anyone.

Sexton's Manchester United attacked on all fronts, spreading the goals throughout the team. While Joe Jordan, who missed almost two months through injury, was their obvious target man, McQueen, Coppell and Macari all weighed in with useful contributions, but they weren't averse to a little help.

When Mickey fell in the Stretford End penalty area during the home match against Ipswich in October, it seemed a harsh decision when the referee pointed to the spot. Harsher still when millions of 'Match of the Day' viewers, later that evening, were treated to a close-up of the United man winking at the camera as he lay prostrate on the Old Trafford turf. The shot was to remain a famous part of the programme's title sequence – an early example of TV's ability to bring the viewer the 'inside story', to take us closer to the action, but it also gave Jimmy Hill something to get his teeth into.

Hill, a tigerish, opinionated pundit even then, used Thomas as an example of a malaise which he saw creeping more and more into the English game – the professional who pretended to be fouled. In other words a diver, a cheat. This offended Hill's – and Ipswich fans' come to that – sensibilities and Mickey became the centre of a row in the press, claiming that it was a 50-50 ball and that the Ipswich defender knocked him over.

Knowing Thomas, it wasn't inconceivable that his wink at the camera was simply a reaction to United's impending shot at goal – Ashley Grimes securing the points from the spot – at a time when United were going through something of a goal drought, just three goals in six games. Grimes and Lou Macari needed all the help they could get. When Jordan returned, he made an immediate impact and United chased Liverpool all the way for the League Title.

Mickey had been at United a year now and was finally beginning to feel at home. He still found life in the Old Trafford goldfish bowl hard to handle, but he realised it was helping his international ambitions at a time when the Welsh were involved in crucial games.

'I hope I never have to choose between club and country, because I love playing for both. But if I did, United would just get the vote.' he said. 'It's a tremendous feeling going out in a United shirt and there's always a big crowd to watch us, home or away.

'When I first turned up for the Wales squad as a Wrexham player, nobody knew who I was. But they all know me now. Well, it sounds a lot better when you say you play for Manchester United doesn't it?

'I'm sure we can keep up this good start to the season because the support of our fans has helped us turn on some fine performances at home and we're picking up points away, too. Once you get a run going, the players start to believe they can do it and other teams don't find us easy to beat.'

It didn't prove to be the case in the FA Cup. Any hopes the players had of returning to Wembley were dashed at the first hurdle with a frustrating third round battle against Tottenham that went to a replay before Spurs sneaked a 1-0 win at Old Trafford. Purists complained it was a shame the two big clubs had met so early on, but Tottenham were delighted to avenge a League Cup defeat at White Hart Lane back in September.

Mickey took a whack on the ankle at Molineux in February and missed six games, but he returned to put in thirty-five appearances and his eight goals were valuable too. So valuable that United went into the final weekend of the season needing to get a point at Elland Road to keep Liverpool in their sights and overhaul them if they slipped up. Leeds United got their revenge on Mickey and won 2-0. It didn't matter. Liverpool walloped Villa 4-1 to lift the trophy with a vastly superior goal difference. Mickey was tired, but he duly reported for the Welsh squad preparing for the Home Internationals.

If Mickey was having trouble coping with the pressures at Old Trafford, they didn't appear to originate on the pitch although he confessed he still held many of his team mates in awe.

'There are occasions when the other players make me feel inferior with the things they can do,' he laughed. 'When I was at Wrexham I went out every week knowing I was going to be the star player, but here I come well down the list.

'I'm not one of the exciting players who the crowd come to watch, but I'm happy to do my job for the other players. My task is working and running for the others.'

His consistency in the first two seasons had been remarkable and the main pressures now weighing on him were those of his troubled marriage. Things weren't going well on that front, and Debbie wasn't making any secret of it. Any Manchester United player in marital difficulty was seen as fair game, especially by the Sunday tabloids, and with Debbie's glamorous background providing plenty of sexy photographs, the papers were quick to sniff a bust-up. Safe to say, the four girls who'd finished above Debbie in the Miss Wales contest would have killed for this kind of publicity. But Mickey put on a brave face and tried his best to present a very different picture.

'I like the quiet life,' he said. 'I'd rather be working on my garden or walking along the beach with my wife than sitting in some pub. The only thing with that is that I don't get to spend much time with the lads socially. But I'm a homely person.'

Everyone involved at the club, and Dave Sexton in particular, knew the 1980-81 season was a hugely important one. Having finished runners-up last season, the fans now demanded their team go one better and put them back where, they believed, they belonged. They had to win the First Division championship, or a cup or two at the very least. The club was like one big pressure cooker and one win in the first five games wasn't the sort of form that was going to see them repeat the last season's near miss.

True, they weren't getting beaten very often, and despite his private life, Mickey, along with Lou Macari and Steve Coppell, seemed to be putting in another storming season. But big Joe Jordan didn't really hit a run of form until November and by then, mindful of the fate of his predecessors, Sexton had gone out on a limb to sign striker Gary Birtles from Nottingham Forest for a whopping £1,250,000. Birtles would play twenty-five league games that season and fail to score in any of them – a record that would ultimately cost Sexton his job – and yet the hyped-up striker made an incredible first impression on the players when he arrived. He turned up at The Cliff to meet his new team mates wearing blue satin trousers and bright red shoes. It was a look that Gordon McQueen described as 'way out gear'.

Cup success eluded United as well with early exits from the FA and League Cups while they could count themselves unlucky to be knocked out of the UEFA Cup by Widzew Lodz on the away goals rule. Sexton was under pressure, but he remained calm.

'Quite frankly I am not interested in how many people do or do not rate us as contenders,' he told *Shoot* magazine in November. 'At this stage of the season such speculation is nonsense. The great attraction of our football is the uncertainty. I doubt if people really realise the fact that we have a very young team, and one which is getting younger all the time. I introduced young Mike Duxbury into the side recently and the boy did remarkably well. He is just one of many youngsters, and now we have added Gary Birtles. I never thought Forest would let him go and we are delighted to have him, even at £1.5million. He will add the goalscoring touch we have previously been lacking.'

New Leeds boss, Allan Clarke, stirred things up by suggesting that Manchester United were now a great club in name only and should get on with proving themselves and forget past glories. He could have been talking about his own club.

By now Mickey and Debbie were living apart. They tried to keep it quiet, at least from the press, but one night, Mickey and his brother were travelling to Colwyn Bay in Mickey's Rover when it ploughed through a hedge. They were badly shaken up but instead of heading for the couple's bungalow in Rhyl to seek help, Mickey travelled on to his mother's house in Mochdre.

Mickey picked up a niggling injury at Leicester in February and apart from a brief three-match return it was to be the end of his season. The break gave him a chance to sort out his home life and come March, Mickey and Debbie were back together again. Debbie had sent her husband on his way by throwing his precious video gear on to the lawn of their bungalow and she followed this by kicking in a glass door, not a good idea when you're bare-footed. Debbie was taken straight to hospital to have twelve stitches put into the wound. She was still just nineteen, but she admitted her behaviour had been 'ridiculous'.

Debbie complained that when Mickey wasn't playing he was watching himself on TV, but occasionally she'd offer her own match verdicts as the couple sat in front of the screen.

'Oh, I don't have to worry about her giving an honest opinion,' smiled Mickey. 'She's more critical than me but watching on video helps me see when I'm not running and working as I should. I even watch the video of the Cup Final because it brings back memories of one of the best days of my life, but I often switch it off just before Arsenal score that late winner. If I see that it reminds me how sick I felt at the time.'

The couple were pictured in the papers walking their new baby, little Aaron, along the beach, just a stone's throw from the Marine Hotel. They spoke candidly of the pressures they'd been under since the 'secret' wedding, with Debbie revealing to the *Sunday Mirror* that her seventeen-hour labour had not gone well and that doctors had later confessed that she and the baby had almost not made it through. The birth was followed by months of depression as the young mum struggled to cope with a baby and a footballing husband playing for Manchester United. Mickey was also still recovering from that crash and was depressed that his Cup Final medal had been stolen. Things weren't great.

'I've been lucky to have been in the first team all the time I've been at United,' admitted Mickey. 'But there is always someone challenging for your place. If I had to go in the reserves for a while and fight for my first team spot, I'd get my head down and get on with it. I've already signed an extra year on my contract, which means I've got another four years here at least and I would be happy to stay here for life.'

For their part, United had slumped alarmingly after Christmas. They lost at home to Leeds and followed it with a humiliating defeat at Maine Road. Only a run which saw them win their last seven matches hoisted them into a respectable eighth place. But respectable wasn't good enough at Old Trafford and on Friday May 1, Sexton was on his way.

The previous day the players had noticed something was wrong. The manager hardly spoke a word to them all morning and he left to attend a board meeting that afternoon. But they were stunned to hear the news when Martin Edwards called the seventeen first team squad members together to explain his reasons for the sacking. Ray Wilkins and Gordon McQueen went on record criticising the decision and pointing to the crippling injuries that Sexton was forced to contend with, while the crowd vented their anger on Birtles, who couldn't even find the net in those last seven games. Nobody among the playing staff felt they'd really done themselves justice. They were all looking over their shoulders now.

Once more it was all change at the club. The directors reasoned that a manager more in the mould of Docherty might do the trick and rouse both players and fans. They couldn't have picked a man better suited to that job than Ron Atkinson. Ron, manager at West Bromwich Albion, was as flash as they came; gold jewellery pouring off him. He had the reputation of being a big spender and wasted no time in offloading United's cash. He bought Bryan Robson and Remi Moses with him, signed Frank Stapleton and Gordon Strachan and expressed an interest in Everton right back John Gidman. Mickey wasn't sure where he would fit into Big Ron's plans but at least he was fit enough to play against Scotland, England and the USSR in May and show his new boss what he could do.

He went back to Colwyn Bay, jogged along the beach, played with the baby and felt safe again. A few lung-fulls of that bracing air and the world seemed a better place. Mickey spent time with his old pals, trying not to come over as too flash as he told them about life at Old Trafford. It was therapeutic spending so much time at home, but he'd also got back into the groove of life by the seaside and it was with some regret that he packed his bags, kissed Debbie and Aaron goodbye and headed for Heathrow. He hated flying.

It was a reasonably relaxed Manchester United squad that occupied one corner of the departure lounge at London's Heathrow Airport as they prepared to jet off to Kuala Lumpur for a pre-season tour in July 1981. Joe Jordan, Ashley Grimes, Lou Macari and Mickey were playing cards, but the little Welshman couldn't stomach the thought of the long flight and the strange food that, his team mates assured him, was waiting at the other end.

'I didn't fancy it one bit,' he recalls. 'Sammy McIlroy and Jimmy Nicholl had already disappeared so I told the lads I was going home. Ashley Grimes and Joe burst out laughing and told me it was too late because my bags were on the plane. Then Lou and a few of the others bet me a tenner each that I wouldn't do it. Anyway, my bags went to Kuala Lumpur for three months and I walked out of Heathrow with £50 in my pocket. And that was the end of my time at Man United.'

Atkinson moved quickly, but it wasn't simply down to Mickey's disappearing act, as was said at the time. If that had been the case, Gordon McQueen, who made his excuses in advance, Jimmy Nicholl and Sammy McIlroy would all have been on their way. McIlroy, who had just returned from international duty, at least offered an explanation for his actions.

'As a contracted player I realise I've done wrong in putting my family first,' he pleaded. 'But I saw them for just a few minutes at

Manchester Airport between trips and with my eight-year-old son Sammy suffering from asthma I wondered how my wife would cope. So, as the plane was about to take off, I unfastened my seatbelt and went home.'

No such excuses for Mickey who was on his way to Everton, the club he idolised as a kid. It was soon clear that the United midfield was to be made the scapegoat for recent disappointments. Even United's young chairman, Martin Edwards, had the knives out.

'When I started watching United in 1958, I just missed the Busby Babes era, ' he said.

'But by the mid 60s Matt Busby had built another great, exciting team. Tommy Docherty built another exciting team in the 70s and now we urgently need another one to get us into Europe and to draw average gates of 50,000 at Old Trafford. They dipped to 45,000 last season and we made £276,000 more in gate receipts the previous season than in 1980-81.

'Our main priority is to please the supporters. In that respect I think Dave Sexton was a total failure. He was reasonably successful on the field, but we felt his team was not exciting the fans. It is not true that letters of complaint sent to me had anything to do with Dave Sexton's dismissal, but they certainly influenced things. Most of them said they felt United were straying from the standards they had set in the past.

'Of the twenty-five or so home games last season, only five or six were truly enjoyable from a spectator's point of view. It's not necessarily the winning, but the manner in which you win. Sexton spent £4 million in four years, so we have the resources.

The board have only vetoed the purchases of two players in the eleven years I've been with them. Managers are allowed to manage here.'

It made depressing reading for a whole-hearted player like Mickey Thomas. He'd run his guts out for the team, but it wasn't good enough for his chairman. He hid his disappointment at leaving Old Trafford well, but if he thought he was leaving one tough manager behind, he hadn't reckoned with his new boss, Howard Kendall.

4: Frankly, Mr Kendall

Howard Kendall had taken over the helm at Everton in May from Gordon Lee after the Merseyside club had fought a battle against relegation all season. With their neighbours consistently adding silverware to the trophy cabinet on the other side of Stanley Park, it was a job for a single-minded, no-nonsense man. Howard Kendall was the man. A veteran of the club's last championship winning side in 1970, Kendall had formed a holy trinity in the Goodison midfield with Alan Ball and Colin Harvey.

The new Goodison boss acknowledged the emerging talents of Steve McMahon, Kevin Ratcliffe and Paul Lodge, but at thirty-four, he still intended to pull on his famous number four shirt when needed. Kendall wasted no time in showing his more ruthless side, sacking Lee's assistant, Geoff Nulty, and first team coach, Eric Harrison. He brought Mick Heaton with him from Blackburn and let his assistant spell out the facts of life for the players.

'He's fair, but he doesn't like being crossed,' he warned them.

'Not many players step out of line because they know he'll be down on them.'

Mickey Thomas arrived as one of seven new faces at Goodison as part of a £450,000 player-plus-cash deal with John Gidman going the other way. And while full-back Gidman was taking his medical at Old Trafford, Mickey was grinning like a kid with the keys to the sweet shop at Everton.

'I watched my first game of football as a six-year-old at Everton,' he revealed at the time. 'And ever since, I've wanted to play for them.'

The new season's official squad photo saw Mickey on the front row between Joe McBride, about to be dropped, and Asa Hartford, about to leave for Manchester City. These were unstable times at Goodison. Mickey wasn't too forthcoming about the departure from United but he claimed it was for football reasons.

'I was never completely happy in the position I played at United,' he said. 'Dave Sexton always used me wide on the left, almost as a winger, but I don't like playing that way. Howard Kendall has his own ideas about how to use me and what he has made plain is that he wants to see me getting forward into the penalty area and scoring a few goals.'

And on leaving Old Trafford?

'There aren't many places you can go after Manchester United are there? But, in my opinion, I have taken a step in the right direction. Everton are on the way back.'

Mickey's first task as an Everton player was to arrange a tour of the ground for his Dad, Reg.

'I asked the manager's permission to do that straight away. I stood and watched football here with my Dad on the Gladwys Street end for many years.'

Mickey certainly looked set for a long stay. He wasted no time answering a 'Super Focus' questionnaire in *Shoot*. It made entertaining reading.

FULL NAME: Michael Thomas
BIRTHPLACE: Mochdre, N. Wales
BIRTHDATE: July 7, 1954
HEIGHT: 5ft 6ins
MARRIED: Yes, to Debbie
CHILDREN: Aaron, 15 months
CAR: Capri Injection
PREVIOUS CLUBS: Wrexham, Manchester United
JOB BEFORE TURNING PRO: Joined Wrexham straight from school
NICKNAME: Mickey
NEWSPAPER: *Liverpool Daily Post*
FAVOURITE PLAYER: Glenn Hoddle
PLAYERS FOR THE FUTURE: Kevin Ratcliffe and Andy Ritchie
FAVOURITE OTHER TEAM: Wrexham
CHILDHOOD FOOTBALL HERO: Alan Ball
FAVOURITE OTHER SPORT: Tennis
BEST EVER ALL-TIME XI: Banks, Kaltz, Beckenbauer, Charlton, Wilson, Ball, Hoddle, Cruyff, Pele, Law, Best
MOST MEMORABLE MATCH: 1979 FA Cup Final v Arsenal
BIGGEST DISAPPOINTMENT: Not signing for Everton sooner

BEST STADIUM PLAYED IN: Wembley

FAVOURITE FOOD & DRINK: Cornflakes and tea

MISCELLANEOUS LIKES & DISLIKES: Playing with my son, Aaron – Hangers on

FAVOURITE SINGER: Bryan Ferry

FAVOURITE ACTOR/ACTRESS: Jack Nicholson and Faye Dunaway

HOLIDAY RESORT: Marbella

TV SHOW: Benny Hill

BEST FILM SEEN RECENTLY: *The Texas Chainsaw Massacre*

FAVOURITE DAY OFF: The beach with Debbie and Aaron

BIGGEST INFLUENCE ON CAREER: Dad Reggie, PE teacher Richard Dodd and former Wrexham boss John Neal

SUPERSTITIONS: I put my boots on three times before the match

PRE-MATCH MEAL: Cornflakes

PERSONAL AMBITION: To win the First Division with Everton

IF NOT A PLAYER WHAT JOB WOULD YOU DO: Pilot

PERSON YOU'D MOST LIKE TO MEET: Pope John Paul

Presumably if he ever met the Pope, the pontiff and Mickey could discuss *The Texas Chainsaw Massacre*.

By the end of October it had become apparent that Kendall's sweeping changes hadn't worked. He used nineteen players in the first ten games, winning just four of them, and though Mickey had played in all ten he picked up a hamstring strain in the home win over Ipswich. Mickey and fellow newcomer, Alan Ainscow, were criticised for not providing the depth and bite that was sorely lacking in midfield, but it was always going to be difficult to accommodate so many new faces at the same time.

Kendall had begun to reintroduce more established players, many of whom had feared their Everton days were numbered as the new recruits were given their chance. Peter Eastoe, John Bailey and Joe McBride were all given a second chance, but one old boy who failed to survive the shake-up, Asa Hartford, reckoned they would struggle.

'Only keeper Jim Arnold has really helped improve on last season's team,' he reckoned. 'But I'm sure even Howard would admit there's no way they are going to win the League.'

Mickey was struggling with his hamstring injury and Kendall was determined his new acquisition should take time to fully recover. Mickey found it almost impossible to rest. He even claimed he got bored sleeping! He stood up to his manager. It was a mistake, and the last he'd make as an Everton player.

'Thomas let me down, the players and the supporters,' thundered Kendall. 'I was not going to be told by anyone who played in my team.'

Many First Division managers were interested, but it would take a brave man to take a chance on Mickey.

'I fell out with Howard Kendall and it was all my fault,' he admitted later. 'I'd been injured but I considered myself fit and ready to play against Manchester City but Howard wanted me to take a little longer so I'd be ready to face Liverpool the following week in a big derby match. He marked me down for a reserves game in the meantime but surprise, surprise I didn't turn up. I told the manager that I'd never had to prove my fitness before and I wasn't about to start now. At the time, I believed my stand was right but looking back on my decision, I suppose I was too hasty.'

There was a lot of bad blood between player and manager, but Thomas denied reports that he'd claimed forgetting Everton wouldn't be too hard because he'd never enjoyed himself at the club.

'I didn't say that. I love Everton. I stood on the terraces as a boy and it was like a dream come true signing from Manchester United. What I said was that Everton were a part of my past and I had to get on with the job at my next club. I didn't get on with Howard Kendall but that's a different matter.

'I never knew where I stood with him and I don't think I was alone in that. I think he wanted to sell somebody around the time that I was pushed out and I gave him the excuse he needed.'

Mickey, his Everton dream in tatters, was about to make the biggest mistake of his career.

5: The Seagull Has Landed

Mickey sat in the plush surroundings of a smart seafront hotel at Brighton on November 5 1981, and scratched his name at the bottom of another new contract. As his new boss, Mike Bailey, shook his hand and welcomed his new midfielder to the south coast, with a glass of champagne, Mickey turned to Debbie, sat nervously beside him. 'What the hell have I done now?' he whispered.

An hour ago he'd been flying south over his beloved north Wales in a private jet from Speke airport, feeling like a million dollars. Even Debbie had been impressed by the red carpet treatment, but now, as the champagne began to go flat, the reality of their situation began to sink in.

Everton had seen at least a £50,000 profit on the deal, and there was a beach over the road to help the Thomas' feel more at home. But it might as well have been a million miles away from North Wales as far as Debbie was concerned. Mickey knew he was in it, once again, up to his neck.

Chapter 5: The Seagull Has Landed

Seagulls' boss, Bailey, was proving to be a shrewd operator as he plotted Brighton's steady climb from the depths of the First Division. A cool £900,000 brought in with the sale of Mark Lawrenson to Liverpool was helping him considerably in this and in Thomas he hoped to bring some class to his midfield.

By the beginning of December it looked to be working. They'd been knocked out of the League Cup by lowly Barnsley, sure, but they'd climbed to a position of respectability and had begun tackling the malaise that had seemed to affect the club for years. Fans and players alike almost regarded the club as a distraction rather than a serious First Division outfit and Bailey knew he had his work cut out to change things.

Alongside Mickey, Bailey brought in Jimmy Case and Don Shanks and tempted both Steve Gatting and Sammy Nelson away from Arsenal. Mickey was being asked to play a different role again, playing deeper and anchoring the midfield, while his usual position on the left was filled by Neil McNab who had undoubtedly benefited from the Welshman's arrival.

'We must make sure we are never satisfied,' said the manager. 'At the moment it would be all too easy to be complacent. There must always be room for improvement.'

Debbie Thomas was already back in Rhyl and Mickey was racking up a huge expenses bill flying home at £80 a time to keep her happy, trying to persuade her to move south. He could have saved his breath, and the club some money. Mickey had a lot of respect for Mike Bailey but he acknowledged his domestic difficulties off the field within a month of signing.

'My problem now is settling,' he said. 'I had just bought a new house on Merseyside which we hadn't even moved into. I was looking forward to getting out of the hotel that my wife, son and I had been living in. Now I've got all that again. It takes its toll you know.'

It was the understatement of the century. Mickey went on to assess his new club and give another of his famous 'kiss of death' pledges to honour his contract.

'Mike Bailey gets on with the job very effectively,' he said. 'He's building a team quite capable of living with the best. It's a big challenge for me because the set-up at Brighton is nothing like it was at Goodison, but it's a friendly little club and the south coast is a lovely place to live. I've signed a four year contract and have every intention of seeing it out. I want success and Brighton can provide it.'

Trouble was brewing. Debbie simply refused to move from her North Wales home which meant Mickey was flying backwards and forwards twice a week after agreeing a generous 'expenses' entitlement for a limited period. By February, that bill had amounted to £2,000 and the local press had made it public. Mickey responded by claiming he didn't expect the club to pay up much longer but things got worse when instead of flying back south on the eve of Brighton's clash with his old mates at Everton, and to explain a week's absence to an increasingly exasperated Bailey, he phoned the Brighton boss and told him he needed time to think things over. The alarm bells must have been ringing on the south coast.

Mickey never made it for the Everton clash. Instead he went to watch his old mates at Wrexham. Ensconced in North Wales once more he walked along Colwyn Bay and felt the magnetic pull of the place. Why go all the way to Brighton when he could stay here, shut his ears to the increasingly exasperated phone calls from Bailey's staff and hope it all went away. Mickey felt he owed Bailey at least an explanation. He rang him at the ground and told him he wanted to leave. Then he disappeared to Marbella.

A month later Mickey was still facing an impossible dilemma. Leave Brighton or face losing his wife. Debbie was adamant that she was staying put in Rhyl and Mickey had gone AWOL once more. As a result he was dropped for the match at Anfield but turned up to watch only to disappear again immediately after the final whistle. He couldn't have infuriated Seagulls fans and players more if he tried. They were battling for First Division survival and Mickey was swanning about in Rhyl.

His Brighton hotel was passing all enquiries on to the club claiming they had no idea where their famous guest was either. Business appointments were cancelled and despite promising he'd face the music, Mickey failed to catch a flight south from Manchester, thus missing the chance to face Tottenham on the Tuesday. He could see no way out of his situation. He was burying his head in the sand once more and regretting his signing to Brighton just eighteen weeks previously.

Football came into it too, he claimed. Mickey was asked to fulfil a specific role at the Goldstone Ground and with little freedom in his private life the prospect of being shackled on the pitch was simply too much for him to bear. His attacking instincts were positively discouraged with Brighton asking him to set up play from a deeper role than he had been used to. There was only one thing for it. He'd have to move to a club nearer 'home', probably at the end of the season. You wouldn't have to be mad to be the next manager to sign him, but it would help.

Mickey promised to knuckle down but went missing prior to Brighton's 4-1 defeat at Notts County. Things had come to a head and he was suspended by the club for two weeks. The money didn't bother Mickey but Mike Bailey admitted that he felt the Welshman had let everyone at the club down for the last time. The players had even welcomed their wayward colleague back into the fold, sympathising with his problems and acknowledging the contribution he could still make.

The joke in the pubs along Brighton's famous lanes was that Thomas had run away from Brighton more times than local hero, Olympian Steve Ovett.

As the season's end approached it was obvious Mickey wasn't going to remain a Brighton player. But Mike Bailey was now worried that he wouldn't even attract a buyer. He'd only played eighteen games as it was and in an unfamiliar role – one which he hated – he'd hardly won over the Seagulls fans or his team mates come to that.

'The other lads don't get time off but they always welcomed Mickey back as if nothing had happened,' said the Brighton boss. 'They are the ones who have come out of this business with credit. We've all been messed about by Mickey and though we have tried to help him with his problem he hasn't responded and that disappoints me.'

Bailey took a deep breath and a huge gamble and decided to

play Thomas in the last game of the season at home to Ipswich. The idea was to put him in the shop window and try to recoup something approaching the £400,000 they paid Everton for him.

Ipswich fans still hadn't forgotten Mickey's Old Trafford wink and the player knew he would have few friends among both sets of supporters. As the teams ran out, Mickey appeared with two huge wads of cotton wool stuffed into his ears to block out the cat calls, and much worse, that he fully expected. He wasn't let down, but the fans also thought it was hilarious and soon he was playing his natural game and loving every minute of it. The cotton wool blew down the touchline as Thomas played his best game for the club, but it would also be his last.

'I did cause them all sorts of problems,' he says. 'Signing for them was a mistake from the beginning so I decided the worse I behaved, the better chance I had of getting out. I broke the club record for fines after going missing for about four weeks.'

When the 1981-82 season ended Mickey breathed a huge sigh of relief. He shut himself away in Rhyl, refusing even to watch the World Cup on TV. He was mentally and emotionally drained and desperate not to start another season on the south coast. It was never very likely. Enter Stoke City boss, Richie Barker, the man credited with saving Thomas' life, or at least his footballing career.

Mickey was delighted to sign for £200,000 even though he was now on half the wages he received at Brighton. He was declaring to the world that all was rosy again and that the worst year of his footballing life was well and truly behind him.

'Honest, I've reformed at last,' he promised. 'I've packed all my nappies away for good and I can promise that the mad days are well and truly behind me. Football will get no more bother from me. Last season was just a horror story for me and I felt trapped.'

He could now admit how close he came to quitting the game altogether while at Brighton and leaving the country – anything to get away from what seemed an impossible choice between his football and family.

And yet even now, free from his south coast hell, he couldn't settle in Stoke. The pull of Colwyn Bay was too strong for him, and Debbie of course, and he spent a staggering £400 a month on petrol driving between North Wales and the Potteries.

Stoke were never likely to be pushing for the League championship. A well supported, well organised club, they had become known as a team with too many players seeing out the twilight of their careers.

Stoke supporters loved Mickey Thomas but they used to joke that the club was becoming a retirement home for ex-Manchester United players. Mickey was joined in midfield by Sammy McIlroy and that only added to the club's reputation. They played entertaining football, they got the ball forward quickly, and if they were really lucky they might sneak a UEFA Cup spot. Mickey kept his head down and for once got on with his football. In fact he produced some of his best form since his Wrexham days, but behind the scenes things were as wild as ever.

By the end of the season his stormy marriage was over. At least that was what Mickey told reporters as the Stoke favourite finally admitted he wanted a divorce. The couple had been married for four years now and Thomas reckoned with his constant travelling and the endless rows with Debbie, the couple had been together for around eight months of it. Cynics weren't surprised. They pointed out that the couple had only known each other three months when they announced their hush-hush wedding but with Aaron now aged three and a six-month-old daughter Jade on the scene, the couple's separation had been difficult.

They had tried to reconcile their differences but Mickey had finally given up. He claimed a complete clash of personalities meant that they had never really hit it off and everything they did ended in a bust-up. Debbie, not for the first time, was telling a slightly different story. She claimed their separations had been purely down to football and that Mickey had broken a string of promises. The sad truth was that they were both right.

Debbie was quick to get her side of the story across. She claimed Mickey had walked out on her for the last time at the end of the season and cited a disastrous would-be holiday as the final straw. The couple had apparently booked a much needed break in Spain for the family, plus babysitter, and Thomas had even phoned home to check Debbie and the kids were packed and ready to leave and that he'd be there to pick them up at 1.30pm on the big day.

Lunchtime came and went and hours later, with the kids in tears, Debbie was still sitting there waiting. She didn't waste any time. She phoned a removal company and ordered a van immediately, filling it with beds and the children's things and left for her mother's. Mickey, keen to avoid the flak for as long as possible, went to Spain without them.

He was now earning £750 a week at Stoke and Debbie claimed she was expected to manage on just £25. The couple had moved into their new £80,000 house in Stoke the previous Christmas Eve but on Boxing Day Mickey had disappeared again. Debbie filed for divorce and left for three months but Thomas begged her to change her mind. When he paid for her to holiday while he looked after the kids she decided to give him one more chance – it seemed such a lovely gesture. But now she'd washed her hands of him and was living in Rhyl with her parents.

'Mike's vanishing acts have happened regularly during our four-year marriage but he's always come back full of remorse,' she said. 'This time it won't work. He always used me as the excuse for him not settling down but that couldn't be further from the truth. It was he who couldn't stand being away from his mum. If things were difficult he would just run home to mother. It wasn't a wife he wanted but a combination of a mother and a slave. I was last to know about his birding and boozing, but then the wife always is.'

Thankfully, while his marriage crumbled around him, on the field at least, Mickey Thomas was going through something of a renaissance.

Teaming up once more with Sammy McIlroy, and with Mark Chamberlain causing havoc on the wing, Stoke started the season with victories over Arsenal, Birmingham, Swansea and Ipswich. Incredibly Mickey only missed one league game all season. He had a point to prove to himself, to his new manager, and to the Brighton fans who travelled to Stoke to give him some stick on October 16. Mickey scored against them, of course, and Stoke won 3-0.

At the Goldstone Ground at the end of February, almost 15,000 turned out to let Mickey know they hadn't forgotten him. The joke on the terraces was that this was the first time many of them had seen him play. And play he did. Mike Bailey sat shaking his head in bewilderment as Mickey set about orchestrating a 2-1 win for the visitors. He scored the first goal too. He scored at Goodison in April and Stoke rose to the heady heights of fifth place before settling back down to mid-table after failing to win any of their last six games of the season.

The following season they just couldn't sustain that kind of challenge and Mickey reckoned he was taking unfair criticism from the fans after Mark Chamberlain revealed some of the players had been into the manager's office to ask for transfers. He didn't mention any names, of course, but with Mickey's reputation everyone assumed he must be one of the want-away stars.

6: King Of The King's Road

Watching the goings on at Stoke with some interest was Chelsea manager, John Neal. Neal, of course, was the man who took the young Mickey to Wrexham to start his career and he saw the wayward playmaker as the perfect man to boost Chelsea's promotion chances after the crucial Christmas period in late 1983. Neal had instigated something of a purge at Stamford Bridge in the summer and had put together a young, talented squad with enough old heads to direct operations out on the pitch. Chelsea had been suffering from too many big-time Charlies who thought they were better players than the facts suggested, and the fans were impatient for a return to the First Division which they last graced in 1979. As the new season kicked-off, Neal knew that, incredibly, they could have slipped into the Third Division at the end of last season.

'Certain players here had lost all sense of reality,' he said. 'They wouldn't listen when we told them the blunt truth. They lived in a dream world and wouldn't come back to reality. The chairman offered to put up the money to put things right – and you don't hesitate when you're given a chance like that.'

In came John Hollins, Nigel Spackman, Pat Nevin, Kerry Dixon, Eddie Niedzwiecki (from Wrexham) and veteran Alan Hudson, back from the USA. Mickey's great pal Joey Jones was also at the club. It couldn't get much better. Neal paid Stoke £75,000 to add Mickey to the jigsaw, citing his enthusiasm and First Division experience as reason enough to gamble on his errant former pupil.

'There was no way I would have joined Chelsea if I wasn't convinced they'd be promoted,' he said. 'This is the first time I've been out of the top flight since leaving Wrexham and I'm certain Chelsea will be my fifth First Division club. It's tremendous to be working with John Neal again, and Joey and Eddie, but that's really just a bonus. It's the standard of football that means everything to me. Chelsea is a First Division club in attitude, tradition and facilities.'

Mickey had now totalled around £1.5 million in transfer fees. Chelsea was run by chairman Ken Bates and he wasn't so sure the club was doing the right thing. As he drove Thomas to Stamford Bridge in his Rolls-Royce to complete the formalities, he stopped at a set of lights and eyed his new player.

'I've been told by many people that you're trouble,' he purred through that famous white beard. 'But John Neal says he can handle you so I'm taking his word.'

Mickey sat back in the plush leather and just then, noticed a good-looking young girl waving at him and his new employer. 'I'd love to spend a few nights with her,' he chirped. Bates stopped the car again. 'That, young man, is my future daughter-in-law,' he growled. It wasn't the best of starts, but his debut for Chelsea couldn't have gone much better.

Division Two wasn't somewhere Mickey planned to spend any longer than needed as he prepared to face Sheffield Wednesday a week later. Describing it as the most important match since the FA Cup Final defeat with Manchester United five years previously, Mickey felt sure that Chelsea could and would be challenging for the First Division. Chelsea won, Mickey scored twice – much to the annoyance of an unimpressed Wednesday boss, Howard Wilkinson – but also suffered a dead leg and spent three weeks limping around the hotel that was now his home. To the Chelsea fans, Mickey had already become a hero after just one game.

'I scored two beauties against Sheffield Wednesday and I couldn't do a thing wrong as far as the Chelsea crowd were concerned,' he recalls. 'I remember Wednesday's defender, Andy Blair, dishing out loads of stick. I'd had enough, so I went over to him and lamped him one. I knocked him clean out. The ref and the linesman didn't see a thing but the crowd were chanting "one Mickey Thomas". You couldn't get away with that sort of thing today.'

A persistent migraine hadn't helped him settle, and he hated his hotel so much he began sleeping in the referee's room at Stamford Bridge, but the Chelsea man confessed he'd never felt happier. His arrival coincided with another surge up the table and John Neal could feel pleased with himself for a gamble that paid off.

'We were beginning to get a bit stale and it's at that point that I bought Mickey Thomas,' he said. 'I cannot praise this lad enough. He is a marvellous pro, full of enthusiasm, positive attitudes and ability. He has vision, pace, tenacity, inexhaustible energy and can score excellent goals. I think Mickey's arrival was just the tonic we needed and he certainly made the kind of home debut you dream about.

'We'll hit some sticky patches between now and May but we have the players to overcome such games. You have to accept that once you set out your stall to be top, other sides will raise their game and make sure you sweat. We want to play with style and entertain people as well as win promotion. So far we're on course on both counts, so now it's up to us to sustain the effort and give one final effort to give one of the most loyal crowds in the game what they deserve – First Division football.'

Mickey and Joey Jones would often head straight back to North Wales after the match, but the London night life clearly added to the appeal of his new club.

'Of course it added spice to things,' he laughs. 'On one occasion I remember I'd gone to Stringfellows on Sunday night, so of course come Monday morning I didn't feel much like training so I marched straight into the physio and told him I couldn't train as I had the flu. He laughed, "There's fuck-all wrong with you, you're training. Now get changed." I kept up the pretence, so eventually he gave me a thermometer. At this point he left the office to attend to someone else and there was a kettle on the side so I popped the thermometer in and switched it on. I must have let it boil too long because the thermometer blew up! The thing's busted and leaking all over the place, so when the physio comes back, I just calmly handed it back to him. He takes one look at it and shouts, "Fuck me, call an ambulance!".'

But still the old doubts, the old questions were being asked. How long would he stick around this time? What would happen when the pressure built up towards the end of the season? Mickey pleaded his case. He wasn't a bad lad, he just stood up for himself and got a reputation because of it. The Chelsea crowd loved him. That season, the team never lost with him in the side. They were promoted as champions.

As the new season kicked off with Chelsea finally back in the First Division, expectations were high. Kerry Dixon and David Speedie were causing unfamiliar defences all sorts of problems and the confidence among the players was sky high. Mickey was on the bench for the early season visit of Everton – much to the travelling supporters' delight, but just four matches into the new campaign he could hardly sleep with anticipation.

If ever a player was born to stick one over his old club it was Mickey Thomas. He may not always have been able to handle the pressure at Old Trafford as a United player, but he relished the chance to go back there and take on his old team mates on September 5. United's fans wasted no time letting the Welshman know how they felt about his return. You don't walk out on them and their club and get away with it. And with United leading 1-0 after fifteen minutes through a Jesper Olsen half-volley, the cat calls and chants got louder and more vicious.

Mickey tossed them the occasional v-sign, flew into tackles with United's defenders and got involved in a few verbal exchanges, but he saved his crowning glory for the fifty-first minute when he sneaked in to leave Ron Atkinson's defence staring in disbelief to slot the ball past a despairing Gary Bailey.

It was United's fourth draw in a row and Mickey claimed he'd remember the goal for the rest of his life. He also twisted the knife by suggesting his old team would struggle unless they went for a more experienced line-up. Did he mean himself? Surely not.

Mickey was loving it at Chelsea. His football was going through something of a renaissance and John Neal was proving as good as his word and keeping Mickey out of too much trouble. It was man management the hard way, but he was no fool and he knew when to allow Mickey some slack and where to draw the line.

'I was going to London in the car with Joey Jones when we were both at Chelsea and to be honest neither of us fancied going training that day,' says Thomas. 'As luck would have it, we heard there'd been a crash on the motorway so we phoned in and said to John Neal, "Sorry gaffer, we can't make it, there's been a pile up on the motorway, it's blocked solid." He says "Yeah I heard about that on the radio too. Unfortunately it's on the other side of the carriageway you lying twat, now get your arses up here sharpish."'

Chelsea had a great season. They just missed out on that UEFA Cup place, but could be delighted with sixth place. They took further pride by finishing top of the 'London League', unbeaten in eight local derbies and Kerry Dixon earned an England call-up thanks to a staggering twenty-four league goals.

Mickey was loving this new lease of life. He'd gone from being yesterday's man at Stoke to Second Division champion and now top six First Division player. Injury had restricted him to just twenty-six appearances, but he'd finished the season strongly, and if he allowed himself a moment to reflect on his upturn in fortunes – and John Neal's help in steering clear of the more distracting aspects of his off-field activities, it wouldn't last long. Life was about to deal him another bizarre hand.

John Hollins took over the helm at Chelsea when John Neal underwent heart surgery in June and Mickey travelled to Norway with the Welsh squad for a friendly ahead of the vital World Cup qualifier with Scotland in September. With John Neal out of the picture, Mickey watched as Mickey Hazard, a similar player to himself, arrived. He didn't disappear to Colwyn Bay or hit the bottle, but determined to knuckle down and prove his worth to Hollins. Three weeks later, Mickey broke his jaw in a pre-season friendly. He did make it back for the Wales v Scotland match but failed to regain his place in the Chelsea line-up. New boy Mickey Hazard was preferred. Thomas packed his bag and signed for bottom-of-the-table West Bromwich Albion two weeks later for £100,000.

7: Bored In The USA

If there were ever any doubts as to Mickey Thomas's lack of judgement, his move from Chelsea to West Bromwich Albion for £100,000 at the end of September 1985 confirmed it. West Brom, now Mickey's seventh club, were already rooted to the foot of the First Division and sleep-walking their way through the club's worst ever season in the top flight. By the time Mickey arrived many 'Baggies' fans had already stopped going to games, the fare on offer was that bad.

'I love a challenge and I'm sure I can get them off the bottom of the table,' said Mickey. 'They're too good to be down there.'

His debut against Coventry came a week after West Brom had been smashed 5-1 by one of his old clubs, Manchester United. His past association with United was immediately held against him by some sections of the West Brom support and when Coventry put three past keeper Tony Godden, it was the last straw. Mickey wondered, not for the first time, what he'd let himself in for. Worse was to come however. Johnny Giles, the manager who'd signed him earlier that week, got the sack after Mickey's first game. Talk about bad luck!

Mickey made twenty consecutive appearances, the only bright spot of which was doing the double over great rivals, Birmingham City. The other two games, count them, that they won were against Southampton and Watford. Mickey failed to score while he was at the Hawthorns, but he wasn't alone in that in a midfield that rotated around Steve Hunt, Tony Grealish, Steve McKenzie, Martin Dickson, Andy Thompson, Darren Bradley and, of course, Mickey himself. A young Carlton Palmer was confined largely to the subs' bench waiting his chance.

Nobby Stiles, the famous old England and Manchester United warrior, took over the hot seat but evidently he didn't fancy Mickey's style. West Brom needed to battle to have any chance at all of staying up and while Mickey would chase and run all day long, his size alone made it impossible for him to intimidate opponents. Stiles needed someone more like himself. Mickey, the player, was a luxury they couldn't afford in a relegation dog-fight and he was loaned out to Third Division Derby County until the end of the season.

Mickey could certainly pick them. While Derby was well within striking distance of North Wales, the club had seen the Inland Revenue issue a winding-up petition against them the previous year. Derby owed the tax man £132,000 and couldn't even hand over Telford United's share of an FA Cup gate. Robert Maxwell, the disgraced – and deceased – tycoon and Oxford United chairman, began taking an interest and put a rescue package together with his son as chairman. Mickey played nine games for the Rams. Twenty-nine league games for two different clubs and no goals, it wasn't Mickey's most memorable season. He needed a change of scene. He'd always fancied trying his hand in America. Now seemed as good a time as any.

The trouble with people who like to disappear now and again when things get too hot to handle is that eventually, everyone knows where you're hiding. If Mickey Thomas disappeared from Brighton, Manchester United, or from international duty, it was a safe bet you could always track him down in Rhyl, Colwyn Bay, Rhos-on-Sea, or back home in Mochdre. Even here, things weren't as simple as they used to be. Mickey was an international superstar now, he'd played for Manchester United and Everton.

The people of Colwyn Bay had always left him alone and respected his privacy. They were delighted that one of their own was so successful in a high profile sport, but now they began to make one or two demands themselves. Perhaps Mickey would like to put in an appearance at this school fête, take a look at this local team, meet his old mates for a drink. It wasn't the same pressure as running out in front of 50,000 screaming United fans at Old Trafford, but it was still pressure. Wouldn't it be great to go somewhere, play football, get paid well and yet be anonymous?

In the mid 1980s there was somewhere just like that – North America. American football was in a strange state. The North American Soccer League, or the NASL as it was called, had finally collapsed in 1985 after just seven years. The game had rallied in the late 70s and 'soccer' was now being billed as the 'sport of the 80s' in North America. And yet, just as the sport finally seemed to be coming to terms with balancing the huge import of ageing foreign stars – many of whom were English – with the development of home-grown talent, the clubs began to fold with alarming regularity.

Some English players became victims of the decline. QPR star Tony Currie, famously signed for Toronto Nationals for £60,000 only to find himself out of work eight weeks later when the first indoor league folded. Bryan Robson, guaranteed superstar status if he ever decided to play in America, sent out a warning to his colleagues.

'My fear is that other British players could suffer the same fate. I warn any player to think twice about going to the States, there are other countries that offer rich pickings for a star footballer.'

Too many players treated America like a well-paid holiday, while the clubs were largely run by people with no knowledge of the game. The American news media hated football. American schools and colleges had embraced the game eagerly, but there has always been a belief in the States that games that don't require hand-eye co-ordination are inferior. Baseball, Basketball, American football, all required it. 'Soccer', the old school would argue, was just a bunch of guys kicking a ball around. Where was the skill in that?

There was a real desire in North America and Canada to get the game organised along professional levels, but in two such huge countries it was a mammoth task and one that looked to have failed by the time Mickey Thomas began thinking it might be just the place for him. It seemed an attractive proposition.

A nervous Mickey Thomas contemplates his debut for Wales v West Germany, 1977

Now at Manchester United, Mickey gets hold of the ball
at Old Trafford, against Arsenal, February 1979

Foiled by Crystal Palace keeper John 'Budgie' Burridge, November 1979

Mickey fires one in with that famous left foot, against Ireland in Cardiff, May 1980

£200,000 saw Mickey join Stoke City in the 1982/83 season, the first of three spells for the club

Mickey prepares to face mighty
Brazil in Cardiff, June 1983.
The game finished a 1-1 draw

Another 1-1 draw in Cardiff. This time against Yugoslavia, December 1983

Mickey arrives at
Chelsea in 1984. The
club clinched the
Second Division
Championship without
him tasting defeat

Christmas 1984 and
Mickey is already
thinking of his next move

Mickey and Gordon 'the 'tache' Davies celebrate a goal against Manchester United, but United run out 3-1 winners, December 1984

Mickey's most famous goal: a twenty-five-yard screamer to equalise for Wrexham v Arsenal in the FA Cup third round, 4 January, 1992

Wrexham's Cup heroes: Thomas and the winning goalscorer
Steve Watkin can't believe they've knocked out Arsenal

Ten days after the Arsenal game, Mickey appears at Wrexham Magistrates
Court to be charged with distributing counterfeit £10 notes

Warrington Crown Court, July 1993. Mickey gets eighteen months for passing dud tenners to Wrexham YTS lads

Many of Mickey's old team mates from Manchester United had already tried their luck in the NASL and they'd tell great stories about good money, fantastic apartments, sunshine, girls, and a bit of football. Jimmy Nicholl had spent three years playing for Toronto Blizzard before heading back across the water to Sunderland, as had Jimmy Greenhoff. Gordon Hill, who Mickey had replaced in the United team, played for Chicago Sting and then Montreal Manic. Even Welsh boss Mike England had starred for Seattle Sounders – and been picked for the League's First All-Star team four times. Mickey's footballing hero, Alan Ball, had tried his hand with Philadelphia Fury and Vancouver Whitecaps, Johnny Giles, Charlie George, Bobby Moore, Rodney Marsh, Geoff Hurst, George Best, Peter Beardsley, Kevin Hector, the list went on and on.

Alan Hudson had also enjoyed a fantastic spell with the Sounders and when he returned to Chelsea as a team mate of Mickey's he would talk long into the night about the brilliant lifestyle and the opportunities in the USA for a sociable, easy-going player. Hudson was one of the original 70s 'mavericks', players who despite their talents never quite made the impact on the game they felt they deserved. They also liked a drink. Mickey Thomas, probably the first, and last, Welsh 'maverick', had never forgotten Hudson's high recommendation of life across the Atlantic. West Bromwich Albion recouped £35,000 and Mickey was on his way.

It was a strange footballing world of seasons that lasted between October and March, where play-offs decided the final placings, goalkeepers wore helmets and Ron Futcher could be joint second top goalscorer in the entire league. They played with an orange ball, big goals, small shorts and six-a-side. Essentially it was still a place to go to when managers in England didn't want you anymore.

The Major Indoor Soccer League, or MISL, had been running alongside the NASL, but following the demise of its big brother in 1985, when the NASL was down to its last nine clubs, the MISL became the only place for aspiring American players and the crowd-pulling foreign imports needed to boost the finances. The crowds averaged around 8,000. Even here times were hard. Many clubs had relied on summer tours of English clubs to help boost crowds but following the Heysel Tragedy, where Liverpool and Juventus fans fought and thirty-nine Italian fans were killed when a wall collapsed, the ban on English clubs playing abroad applied in the USA too. There were ways around that, of course. In the summer of 1986, Queens Park Rangers – disguised as the Tampa Bay Rowdies – played a team comprising former NASL players in front of a crowd of 35,000 on Independence Day in the Tampa Stadium.

Mickey joined the Wichita Wings, America's oldest professional soccer team, in 1986. They had been playing indoor soccer at the Kansas Coliseum just North of Wichita since 1979 and were now one of six teams, along with Tacoma Stars, Kansas City Comets, San Diego Sockers, St Louis Steamers and the Los Angeles Lasers in the Western Division of the MISL. Each club played a total of fifty-two games, the top four from each division going into the divisional semi-finals followed by the combined semi-finals. The two top clubs, one from the Western and one from the Eastern, divisions would then play a five-game match to decide the overall Champion. In 1986/87 the Eastern Division comprised Cleveland Force, Baltimore Blast, Dallas Sidekicks, Minnesota Strikers, Chicago Sting and the newly reactivated New York Express.

It all sounded exciting and glamorous to Mickey and he explored his new home and the surrounding area with some relish. Wichita, the largest city in Kansas, was originally built up by early settlers in the mid 1800s around a traditional meeting place for native American Indians. The Wild West flavour of the city's origins is helped in no uncertain manner by the fact that William Bonney, better known as Billy The Kid, was born there and that the world's biggest Western Wear store, 'Sheplers' is still booming. Those early settlers shared their adventures with the Comanche and Cheyenne Indians and Mickey would have appreciated the city's early reputation as a raucous one full of saloons and card houses.

Modern Wichita is based around the aerospace industry, with Boeing, and Learjet among the city's major employers. Wichita is also the home of Pizza Hut, where brothers Frank and Dan Carney borrowed $600 from their mother to launch what is now an international corporation.

And so it was here that a Welsh soccer star – though the locals insisted on calling Mickey English – touched down and began his indoor career. The anonymity he enjoyed driving around the city was a breath of fresh air. It was a long way from Mochdre, but there was no real pressure playing in the MISL and his quick feet suited the indoor game, nicknamed 'human pinball' by the locals. The club had enjoyed some prominence in the MISL but like St Louis Steamers, was forced to auction off players' shirts in the summer of 1987 in an attempt to raise money to satisfy creditors. Mickey's shirt was among the top earners. The game was being run on fairly modest lines by now but the team bosses believed things would turn around. Soccer was hugely popular in schools and the kids who'd started playing in the early 70s, inspired by the arrival of stars such as Pelé and Franz Beckenbauer, were now paying customers with kids of their own. It made more sense to base the MISL, and plans for a new professional outdoor League, on this core audience.

Manchester United players were always in demand in the USA. The club was one of the most famous in the world and its players – even ex-players – were crowd-pullers wherever they went. Mickey's style and sense of fun on the pitch made him a star and that was exactly what the MISL needed.

'I tried never to spend money on players who were just good players but players who would be crowd-pullers,' explained former NASL president Clive Toye – the man who brought Pelé to America. 'One of our clubs spent $800,000 on a centre-half. Now who the hell spends $800,000 on a centre-half? Good player, sure, but nobody was going to pay money to come and see him play. A lot of money was wasted on foreign players at a time when we should have been diminishing our reliance on them. The influx of new clubs accentuated our reliance on them when we should have been starting to feed more American players into the League.

'Basically, the mistakes were not knowing anything about the work which went into producing a good club, spending too much unnecessary money on foreign players and undertaking the clash between the outdoor and the indoor game. When money didn't bring them success some of the club owners decided it was the game's fault and so they wanted to change the game – change offside, that kind of anti-FIFA attitude.'

Wichita Wings, and other indoor clubs, didn't have to worry about FIFA. The MISL incorporated rules and practices from other games to make itself more attractive. Mickey was amazed in his first game with Wichita when different opponents were facing him every ten minutes. The game was made even faster by introducing substitutes at any time in the game – one player on, one player off, but it came in handy if you were a Welsh soccer exile and you fancied a breather occasionally.

Wichita Wings finished their first season with Mickey in the team in fourth place – remember there were only six teams in the Western Division – but that was good enough to make it into the Divisional semi-finals and five matches against table topping Tacoma Stars. Tacoma came out on top 9-7, 9-1, 3-10, 2-6, 4-2 and went on to contest the Championship play-offs where they lost the best of seven games finale to Dallas. It was all very strange to Mickey but there were compensations. The city was a busy, friendly place and if he fancied a reminder of North Wales and Colwyn Bay he could always drive up to the huge Lake Afton with its fishing and sailing and take in the sights. The City even boasted its own Rugby Union club – the Wichita Barbarians – it was just like being at home.

The 1987–88 season didn't get any better for Mickey and his

Wichita Wings team mates. New York had lasted less than a season back in the MISL and rumours were circulating that other teams might not last the season. The Wings finished one off the bottom after their fifty-six games, losing thirty-three of them, and failed to make the cash-generating semis. When the season ended, with San Diego Sockers beating Cleveland Force for the MISL Title, Chicago, Tacoma and Minnesota all folded. Perhaps this wasn't the promised land after all.

The indoor game was much harder than Mickey expected. Players saw a lot more of the ball and there was no hiding place but he liked it that way. 1987–88 was Mickey's last with Wichita. He'd given it his best shot and enjoyed the experience, but the clubs were all tightening their belts and there was talk of the league featuring its first professional female player. It was time to succumb to the pull of North Wales. He returned to English football with Shrewsbury – about as near to Wales as he could get.

Mickey was installed, on a free transfer, by Shrews boss Ian McNeill, in time for a pre-season trip to Scotland and the official club photograph. Mickey looked fit and happy in the front row. He was raring to play some 'real' football again. As he ran out at Gay Meadow to face Portsmouth on August 27 1988, Mickey knew there were people in the crowd expecting him to disappear soon. Most of the supporters, both home and away, were amazed to see Mickey. They assumed he'd retired or gone AWOL once too often and never returned,. Where had he been for the past two years? Wherever it had been, he'd obviously kept fit. Looking sharp and relaxed, he soon set about the Pompey midfield, raiding down the left when the opportunity arose.

Shrewsbury lost 2-1, but Mickey was back and determined to prove he could play a whole season.

Not that he could keep out of the news. A month after the season started, his stormy relationship with Debbie had erupted on the pages of the Sunday papers. This time they were battling over custody of the kids – Jade and Aaron. According to the *Daily Star*, Mickey claimed Debbie had virtually kidnapped six-year-old Jade from his mother's house in Mochdre. Mickey claimed Debbie was using the kids to barter over who should have the couple's £100,000 house.

'Debbie said she would fight custody if I didn't sign over the house,' Mickey told the paper. 'She will put Jade on the phone and that really breaks my heart. Jade gets hysterical and asks can she come home. I have no intention of handing over the house. It's all I have to show from my football career and she has never done a day's work in her life.

'Any woman who can barter her children for money isn't worth the time of day. Debbie promised me custody of the children because they have always leaned towards me. She just walked into my mum's house, grabbed Jade and took her out to the car shouting. My mother is not very well and there was nothing she could do. I'm praying the divorce judge will ask the children who they want to stay with. I know they will choose me.' Mickey's son was now living with his dad. 'Aaron's a great little chap and has come though all this with flying colours, but he misses his sister a lot. They are very close.'

It seemed harsh on the children's mother. Mickey had just returned from two years in America and now he was claiming their mother wasn't interested in the kids. Football wives the country over sympathised with Debbie, but few people knew the truth behind their divorce battle.

'I'm not claiming to be the Archangel Gabriel,' shrugged Mickey. 'I've done my share of boozing and womanising in the past. But I have never neglected my kids. I love them and they love me. Debbie didn't want to know them when we split up. All she wanted was my money.'

The couple were being beautifully set up by Fleet Street. Three days later, Debbie was posing with happy family shots of her and Jade and putting her side of the story forward – in the same daily paper. Had she virtually kidnapped Jade?

'That's a vicious lie,' she stormed. 'Of course I've not kidnapped Jade. I love her and she loves me. He may have earned good salaries but we never saw any of the money. He left us for eight months without a penny.'

The couple were now living nearby to each other, but divorce lawyers had warned them not to make contact.

With all this going on it's a wonder Mickey found time to train and play regularly with Shrewsbury. But he did. In fact, he was the club's most consistent player by far, racking up forty games in the 1988-89 season – more than any other player. He scored just the one goal – against Birmingham. Blues fans hated the sight of him. Shrewsbury only won eight games that season and were relegated to Division Three, but Mickey was back. Who knows, he would joke in the bar after games, he might have one big move left in him yet.

When the phone call came telling him that Leeds United

wanted to sign him, Mickey concluded someone was pulling his leg. Leeds United? They were managed by Howard Wilkinson, the man who had been less than flattering after Mickey's double strike on his debut at Chelsea had beaten Sheffield Wednesday, then Wilkinson's club. This had to be a joke.

But it wasn't. Instead of lining up with his pals at Shrewsbury to face Reading at Elm Park for the new season, Mickey found himself at St James' Park, Newcastle, wearing the white shirt of Leeds. They'd never replied to his request for a trial back in 1969, but here he was plucked from the Third Division to line-up alongside Gordon Strachan, David Batty, Ian Baird, Bobby Davison and the like. Leeds got stuffed 5-2 and Mickey was subbed, but he was back in the starting line-up the following week for the 2-1 win over Middlesbrough and again for the midweek draw with Blackburn Rovers. Then, as if the Leeds midfield needed any more bite, with Batty snapping at opponents heels, Vinnie Jones replaced Mickey and that was his lot as a Leeds player. He stayed at the club until March 1990 but never played again.

Another loan spell seemed on the cards as the end of season shake-up approached and this time one of his old clubs broke with tradition and invited him back. Mickey rejoined Stoke, the club that had saved his career when he left Brighton. Stoke's under-fire manager was Mickey's all-time hero, Alan Ball. Mickey ran his heart out for the boss and played in the last eight games of the season but City were relegated to the Third Division. He jumped at the chance to sign a one-year deal with Ball, in a summer which saw England's heroics in Italia 90, and knuckled down to help the man he admired so much. A goal on his debut at home to Rotherham got the fans buzzing. Mickey was back, he'd save them. He was voted Player Of The Year. Mickey had looked after himself and was naturally fit, but he was thirty-six now and not everyone at Stoke rated him so highly. Stoke finished fourteenth, Mickey played thirty-eight league games and scored a very useful seven goals. But Alan Ball got the boot and Mickey felt he was forced out too. He wouldn't stay where he wasn't wanted.

At the Victoria Ground, he'd proved to himself that it wasn't always a mistake to go back. He needed a club, why not stick to familiar territory. He made up his mind. It was either Manchester United or Wrexham. The Racecourse had changed a lot since Mickey had been away on his adventures. Both the Plas Coch and Mold Road stands and the terracing in front had been closed by the safety authorities in the wake of the Bradford fire in 1985 and a peek through the closed and rusting turnstiles still reveals the crumbling scene of glorious European nights in the 70s.

But the club remained ambitious and Brian Flynn was building an exciting young team around a few older heads – namely Joey Jones and Flynn himself on occasion. Mickey's would complete the jigsaw. It was like a Wales old-boys reunion but Flynn was sure Mickey could do a job, directing play and pinging those old left-footed passes to his younger charges. If giving him the number five shirt was intended to curb Mickey's desire to prove to everyone how fit he still was, it didn't work. Roared on by his old admirers, Mickey covered every inch of the Racecourse and played twenty-six league games. Mickey carried on playing while the club's famous FA Cup run was sustained – finishing with that hard-fought 1-0 Fourth Round replay defeat at home to West Ham, but by mid-January 1992 charges had been brought against him in connection with forged ten pound notes and it was difficult for him to carry on at the club. He did return for the last two games of the season and was delighted when Flynn agreed to let him return for pre-season training to try to prove he was worth another contract.

When the Wrexham players, YTS lads and a handful of young trialists reassembled in the Racecourse Ground car park in mid-July you could have been forgiven for assuming Mickey Thomas wouldn't be among them. But no. There he was, welcoming new boy Tony Humes from Ipswich and discussing holidays with Joey Jones. Now thirty-eight years old and still wearing his famous number eleven training kit, Mickey was playing his annual pre-season joke – a football stuck up his shirt. He was about to begin his twentieth gruelling pre-season.

As usual, the running was no problem. Pounding Erddig Park was a personal challenge for Thomas. The kids around him may have more of a future ahead of them, but while Mickey could finish among the top runners in the club, he figured, with some justification, that he could always earn another year's contract. The alternative – a life without football – didn't bear thinking about. The year's contract was his, and despite last season's problems, Bryan Flynn had also made Mickey club captain for the forthcoming campaign.

'That was a nice little bonus,' he admitted.

The squad spent the morning running at Erddig, then reassembled after lunch and headed for the playing fields of a local primary school. The club had no training ground of its own and relied on local support for facilities. A few bemused teenagers dozed in the sun, one eye on the exertions of the red-faced footballers in front of them.

Mickey Thomas wasn't so keen. Running on the beach, through the forest, or in a match was one thing, 'interval running' with Joey Jones shouting commands wasn't his idea of fun and he spent a good twenty minutes lacing up a new pair of boots. Ball work was the only one of four supposedly 'compulsory' activities Mickey was interested in.

He ambled over to the spectators to shoot the breeze and tell anyone interested, with a laugh, that his new Adidas 'mouldeds' were bought with crisp £10 notes!

'What they don't realise is that I'm ten/fifteen years older than some of them and I've been doing pre-season for twenty years,' he pointed out. 'It definitely gets harder but I'm definitely one of the fittest because I've always trained right through the summer and that's why I'm still playing.

'The Guinness probably helps but that's only something I've done late on in my career. I've clocked up more than 700 senior matches including fifty-one for Wales and you can't do that if you're a boozer. I think a lot of players have a drink at home, but they don't say anything. It doesn't affect your performance, I can't see anything wrong with it. If it did I'd have to do something – have three pints maybe!

'In fact I didn't drink until I was twenty-four, and it was the pressure of playing for Manchester United which drove me to it. I was never able to cope with that move after seven years at Wrexham. The pressure at Old Trafford was enormous and I couldn't handle it.'

Thomas realised that this could be his last season. He'd even begun seeking out old videos of his best performances.

'I've just started buying tapes because when I was at United we were on TV every week and you just didn't bother videoing them. The best goal I ever scored was at Tottenham and I've got that on tape. Pat Jennings was in goal and it went right in the top corner!'

Better than the goal against Arsenal in 1992?

'Oh yeah,' he laughed. 'I see a lot of Arsenal fans and if I was going to score a goal and score it on TV, I couldn't have scored a better one really. It was one of the highlights of my career, but I always scored against Tottenham, I don't know why. I wasn't very popular when I used to go there.'

And so it was back to Erddig Park, out-running seventeen-year-olds and wondering what the future held. He was delighted to have been given the chance of another season, but as usual just as things looked to be going his way, his world caved in once more. Days before the new season started Mickey met the man with the hammer and screwdriver. But reports of his demise proved premature and he trotted out at the Racecourse on September 12 to face his old mates at Shrewsbury. He played another seven consecutive league games, pulling the strings in midfield, encouraging and inspiring the kids around him, before his injuries took their toll.

Mickey Thomas

Mickey Thomas' last league game for the club kicked off miles from Wrexham, at Colchester United on October 30 1992. He didn't score, but the team won 4-2 and that's what always mattered to the little man from Mochdre. That season, his last in League football, Wrexham were promoted to Division Two.

8: The Road From Mochdre To Wembley

The FA Cup was one of the reasons Mickey Thomas signed for Wrexham in the first place. While he was waiting on that letter from Elland Road for the trial that never happened, Wrexham, who he was with as an amateur, embarked upon one of their most famous Cup runs. Nobody was surprised when they accounted for non-League Spennymoor United in November 1969 and carried on their travels with a win at Hartlepool. But then things got better. Norwich, of the Second Division, away, and another win and then in the hat for the Fourth Round and a reasonable chance of meeting one of the big boys.

In 1970 they didn't come much bigger than Bill Shankley's Liverpool. As the Merseyside giant's name was read out first, midway through the draw, the silence in pubs and homes alike was punctuated by shouts of 'they'll do for us'. When Wrexham came out next, people ran out of their doors to make sure the neighbours had heard the news. Liverpool v Wrexham, at Anfield on January 24. The average crowd at the Racecourse was

around the 8,000 mark and there were players, and young ama-
teurs for that matter, who'd never seen a crowd much bigger.

When Arfon Griffiths led the team out at Anfield, they could
have been forgiven if they'd frozen stiff. 54,096 fans – the biggest
ever to see a Wrexham team play – were packed into the great old
ground, its world famous Kop stretching almost to heaven, a vast
sea of heaving Scousers and their red and white scarves. Bloody
'ell! When they got excited behind the goal, they would tumble
down towards the fence at the front and then, as if by magic, be
swept back up to their previous vantage point, give or take ten
yards. They had come to see their superstar team send the visitors from 'down the road' back to Wales with a headache.

Only nobody told the Wrexham number nine, Ray Smith.
Incredibly, he put the Welshmen ahead, in front of the mighty
Kop, when he met Ian Moir's cross. Wrexham couldn't hold out,
of course, but in the end Liverpool were made to work hard for
the three goals they replied with. It was the stuff of legend and
Mickey Thomas wanted some of it. He signed on the dotted line
two months later.

His own FA Cup debut came in November 1972 in a First
Round replay at the Racecourse against Darlington. Wrexham
won 5-0 and Mickey announced his arrival in the competition
with one of the goals. The following season, injury robbed him
of a hand in another famous Wrexham victory as they defeated
Southampton at the Dell in the Fifth Round after previously
accounting for both Crystal Palace and Middlesbrough. It was
the furthest they'd ever progressed in the competition and in the
mud on the south coast they won a famous 1-0 victory thanks to

a Dave Smallman header. Mickey was on the bench. He never got on. He was there again when the Robins lost 1-0 to Burnley at Turf Moor in the quarter-final.

It only took Wrexham three more years to reach the quarter-final again and this time Mickey was there every step of the way. Burton, Preston, Bristol City – in a replay – and then on to Newcastle United. As usual Wrexham were drawn away but they battled to a well deserved 2-2 draw at St James' Park and brought the famous Magpies back to the Racecourse. In the second minute, Dixie McNeil put Wrexham ahead to the delight of almost 19,000 fans and although Newcastle equalised shortly before half-time, Wrexham still found time to strike another before the break. Newcastle found no answer in the second half and unforced errors and the deadly finishing of Les Cartwright and McNeil saw the Robins stroll into the next round. Amazingly they were soon back at St James' Park, only this time in a replay to face local non-League outfit, Blyth Spartans. More Geordies turned out for this game than had bothered for the Newcastle home match, such was the pull of their victors, and over 42,000 appreciative Tynesiders watched McNeil and Whittle put the Welshmen through.

Mickey Thomas liked the idea of Arsenal coming to Wrexham on March 11, 1978. The two games against Newcastle had shown him he could live with the boys from the First Division and now he'd get his chance to prove it all over again against one of London's most famous clubs. Wrexham even scored twice, but the visitors replied with three and another quarter-final ended in glorious defeat. It was close, and Mickey prayed he might get another shot at the Arsenal.

It would happen sooner than he would ever dream possible. Now a Manchester United player, Mickey's first FA Cup campaign at Old Trafford just went on and on. He missed the opening round against Chelsea in January 1979, but was back to see off Fulham in the Fourth Round, and an awkward away win at Colchester United a few weeks later. Then things got interesting. United were drawn away to Tottenham Hotspur in the quarter-finals and just under 52,000 punters took the long stroll up Tottenham High Road to see Mickey score United's goal in the 1-1 draw. Four days later they were replaying at Old Trafford, an extra 3,500 fans able to watch this one, with United finally making it through 2-0.

Mickey had never played in a semi-final before – the Welsh Cup excepted – but now he'd get the chance to put one over the team he despised as an Everton-supporting kid: Liverpool. The United players didn't exactly feel the venue, Maine Road, counted as 'neutral', but they played their part in a thrilling 2-2 draw and dragged their tired bodies up to Goodison Park for the replay. Mickey was in seventh heaven.

Playing at Goodison Park, against Liverpool. Wow! He had to win this one. His team mates didn't let him down and Jimmy Greenhoff scored the only goal of a tense affair. That just left the matter of the Final at Wembley Stadium on May 12.

United played two games in the week leading up to the Final – fixture congestion is nothing new – a timid display away to West Brom and an easy win at home to Wolves. The next day they took the coach to London.

It rained in north London the day before the Final but come

2.50pm on the 12th when the team took to the hallowed turf, Wembley was wearing her usual big occasion welcome of bright sunshine. United had emerged from the home dressing room looking determined, and Arsenal, in their changed strip of yellow and blue, joined them in the tunnel. Some of the players shook hands, others ignored each other and blinked out through the mouth of the tunnel where they could see the Manchester United supporters massed behind the far goal. They got the word to walk, and set off, studs rattling on the concrete, out of sight of the crowd.

Dave Sexton looked relaxed, as always, as he emerged along-side Gunners boss Terry Neil and was then followed by his captain Martin Buchan – a cross between Bobby Moore and Nick Berry – Gary Bailey, Jimmy Nicholl, Arthur Albiston, Joe Jordan, Gordon McQueen, Lou Macari, Steve Coppell, a more nervous than usual Mickey Thomas and finally the Greenhoff brothers walking side by side. Arsenal's Brian Talbot couldn't believe his luck. This was his second successive Final with different clubs. His Ipswich winners medal was given pride of place at home, reward for last year's defeat of his new club, Arsenal. The London outfit kicked off and Mickey was straight into the action, flicking on a clearance from Albiston immediately beneath the Royal Box. His second touch, another header, reached Jimmy Greenhoff as the crowd sang 'When the Reds go marching in', but it was a cautious, tentative start all round. The players seemed surprised at the greasy surface and they slipped and lost their footing regularly in the early exchanges.

Suddenly United counter-attacked at pace and McIlroy hit a

lovely diagonal ball for Mickey to run on to. He attacked the edge of the Arsenal box, but his hurried shot cannoned off of Pat Rice for a throw in. He collected the ball again from the throw and, realising he was penned in by the flag, cleverly worked a corner off the same defender.

On twelve minutes, Liam Brady picked up the ball in the Arsenal midfield, skipped past Macari and slipped inside Mickey, leaving Nicholl in his wake. His pass to Stapleton was directed to David Price who cut the ball back from the byline to see a combination of Talbot and Alan Sunderland fire the ball into the unguarded net. 1-0 to the Arsenal, as they say. The Arsenal pair would still be disputing who'd got the final touch when the second half kicked off.

But for now it was still early. Mickey hit a fine cross towards Greenhoff then deflected a pass into the path of McIlroy who should have done better than hit it straight at Pat Jennings in the Arsenal goal. Liam Brady was already showing ominous signs of taking complete control of the midfield and Mickey's regular, lunging two-footed tackles were meat and drink to the classy Irishman. He skipped past his opponent leaving him baffled and on his backside.

But Mickey's nerves were settling and while he wasn't getting much time, or seeing a lot of the ball, he got in a tigerish tackle on twenty minutes to rob Pat Rice. Rice was back at him quickly and Mickey executed a neat little drag-back before just failing to nutmeg the right-back in the same move. The United number eleven was getting into some good positions now and McIlroy in particular was finding him with the ball. But too often, Rice or

Willie Young would just get enough on the ball to frustrate Mickey's intended pass.

He flew in two-footed again as Rice advanced down the wing but he came out with the ball and no foul was given. Then it was McIlroy's turn to break down the left but he was cynically checked by the Arsenal captain who earned the first yellow card of the game. The tackles started to fly thick and fast now, Brady on Macari, Young through the back of Jordan, Rix on Coppell and Talbot on anyone who got in his way.

With half an hour on the clock, Jordan dummied a cross from the right. Mickey was the only player alive to it, diverting the ball cleverly with his head into the path of Greenhoff who watched in agony as his snap shot shaved the bar. Mickey may not have possessed the passing ability of Lou Macari or the change of pace of Steve Coppell but he was getting more and more involved on his first Wembley appearance and clearly relishing it.

He was playing relatively deep today. Albiston had a tendency to want to hit the ball long and he often looked for Jordan or Greenhoff to attack the space behind Pat Rice. Mickey could then get isolated when United had the ball and he would track back as far as his own penalty area if it meant more chance of seeing the ball.

It was getting even warmer out there on the pitch now and Mickey was getting through a phenomenal amount of work. His busy little stride was taking him all over the pitch but it may have been that he was keen to receive the ball in an area where the turf was truer. Curiously, the length of the famous Wembley pitch in front of the Royal Box was bumpier than usual – a legacy of the fact that it was dug up to accommodate Speedway races at the time. The ball would skip and jump as it was rolled along the supposed 'hallowed turf' and that wasn't great for ball players. It could make you look stupid if you weren't careful. On the other hand, United had been having problems with their own pitch so Mickey was used to it. Coppell would find it more of a problem when they switched flanks in the second half.

Mickey tracked an ambitious run from the young Arsenal centre-half David O'Leary, launching a perfect slide tackle and winning the throw in. His tackling had to be snappy and accurate because he always seemed to end up on his backside. Only Brady seemed too elusive for his somewhat limited technique – but then he was too elusive for everyone. With ten minutes remaining of the first half, Gordon McQueen had the ball in the back of the Arsenal net. It was disallowed, presumably for a foul on Jennings, but TV replays showed the big Scot had actually knocked the ball in with his hand.

Mickey was released on the left again but as he headed for goal and tried to cut the ball back behind McIlroy's dummy run, it cannoned off the Irishman's heels and Arsenal set off on the counter attack. Rice flew into the empty space behind Thomas, passed to Brady who once more dribbled effortlessly into the box before chipping exquisitely to the far post where he'd spotted an unmarked Frank Stapleton. 2-0 to Arsenal on forty-three minutes and United were in trouble.

Tempers were fraying and McIlroy and Talbot were involved in a heated exchange that saw the United man drop his forehead on to the bridge of Talbot's nose directly in front of referee Ron

Chalice. Perhaps his unfeasibly large white collar had obscured the official's view of an obvious yellow card offence. Today it would have been red. Half time.

The band of the Royal Marines couldn't get on the pitch quick enough, and likewise, Dave Sexton needed to get his team firing again. Arsenal had had three good chances and scored from two of them; Stapleton's acrobatic overhead kick sailing over the bar. United needed to bring Greenhoff and McIlroy into things more as Jordan was being shepherded well by Willie Young.

United kicked off the second half in blazing sunshine, a 'Jim'll Run The Greenhoff Wembley' banner leading the United rallying call. Joe Jordan rose to meet a Nicholl cross but missed it and it dropped to an unsighted Mickey and bounced past him out of danger. He popped up in his own box and took two slide tackles in quick succession to see the ball safely out for a throw in. On fifty minutes Mickey wriggled past Rice on the byline and with United players in the box, drove the ball against a defender. If he could only get that final ball on target, United might find a way back into the game.

Brady set off again and Mickey was determined to halt his progress. He had two bites at the wiry Irishman, but didn't even touch him. Brady was threatening to steal the show while Mickey seemed to be struggling more now to make an impact. He was defending as much as raiding down the left but when he did win the ball and looked up, Jordan and Greenhoff were finding it increasingly difficult to stay in touch with him and to make themselves available for the pass.

Ten minutes into the half, Mickey had remembered some

good old-fashioned schools football advice and decided to go looking for the ball as it wasn't coming to him. He popped up on the right wing this time and made a chump out of Brady, winning a tackle, feinting to go back towards his own goal before spinning and leaving Brady for dead. United were coming into things more as they pushed men forward, but that allowed Rix to set off on a brilliant close control dribble that took him from the half way line to the penalty area.

Mickey wasn't finished with Liam Brady yet. Together with Jordan he pressured the Arsenal man into losing possession. Then, as Brady tried to nick the ball away, Mickey executed a perfect drag back, cut inside Graham Rix and laid it off to Albiston. His best work was being done under the nose of the manager, and on TV, Jimmy Hill was picking him out, rather generously perhaps, as United's best player. With ten minutes remaining, Mickey's big day looked like fizzling out. He nipped through the well-drilled Arsenal offside trap as McQueen clipped a clever ball over the top, but Jennings was alive to it and came racing out to snuff out the danger. Mickey showed his frustration by cutting down Pat Rice after diving in wildly and being turned.

Five minutes left now and Arsenal brought on the impossibly long-legged Steve Walford in place of David Price. Brady was holding the ball up well, letting precious seconds tick by, inviting the challenge from his increasingly frustrated opponents. He was playing with them, it was almost too cruel. A hopeful long ball saw O'Leary clatter into the exhausted and ineffectual Greenhoff outside the box and the resulting free-kick was hit more in hope than anything else. Coppell knocked it across the box to Jordan who spun and hit it back along the six-yard box. McQueen, still annoyed that the free-kick hadn't arrived on his head, couldn't believe his luck. He turned it in like a seasoned goal-poacher. 2-1, but it was too late now, surely.

Arsenal needed only to keep their nerve and run it into the corner. Greenhoff picked up a loose ball, laid it off to Macari, to Nicholl, back to Albiston, to Nicholl again, into Coppell then a lovely pass slipped through to McIlroy on the edge of the box. The crowd held its breath. McIlroy advanced and dragged the ball cleverly inside David O'Leary's challenge. The Manchester United bench were on their feet. McIlroy poked it through Walford's legs as the substitute launched himself at the ball. Arsenal fans screamed. Jennings raced out of his goal as Willie Young came across to save the day but McIlroy got there first – just – to squeeze the ball past them and watch it roll sedately into the far corner. 2-2, unbelievable.

Mickey Thomas was the first player to reach Sammy. All those years training on the beach at Colwyn Bay had finally paid off. He shook McIlroy by both shoulders as the rest of the team piled in from behind. They'd done it, pulled back a two-goal deficit in the FA Cup Final with two minutes left on the clock. Both sets of fans were in tears. Arsenal couldn't believe they might lose their second successive Cup Final. United just couldn't believe any of this was really happening. But they needed to clear their heads and prepare for the physical, and mental, challenge of thirty minutes extra time. Lou Macari looked around the pitch and was convinced the United players had the legs to come again. 'We can win this one,' he told himself.

A dejected Arsenal restarted the game as the referee checked the time with both linesmen. Back to Sammy Nelson, hit long towards Stapleton who chested it down and knocked it off to Brady in space. One last effort from the Irishman as he set off and ghosted past Macari and then arrogantly shook off Mickey's desperate lunge. As Buchan came to meet him on the edge of the box he rolled it wide to Rix who sent in his cross. Alan Sunderland was unmarked on the far post but he expected Gary Bailey to pluck the ball out of the sky. He didn't, he stretched and missed it. The ball dropped as Arthur Albiston arrived behind Sunderland but the Arsenal man had only to knock it into the empty net and Arsenal had won the Cup. He set off to celebrate – man, moustache, and curly perm in perfect harmony.

Joe Jordan still had time to loop a header into Pat Jennings' safe hands, but Mickey wouldn't get another touch. With two minutes added to time already played, the referee blew the whistle. Some of the players swapped shirts. Mickey wasn't letting anyone have his. Darker red now, with the sweat of ninety minutes non-stop running beneath a blazing May sun, its over-sized number eleven stretching from beneath his hair to the waistband of his shorts, Mickey Thomas would keep hold of it, thank you very much.

When the United players trudged wearily up to the Royal Box to collect their losers' medals from Prince Charles, Steve Coppell made as if to throw his away. Mickey wouldn't have to. His would be stolen a few months later. Wembley is no place for losers. Nobody wants to talk to or look at you. The biggest Cup

Final in the world and you've lost. There was nothing to do but go out and get rat-arsed. Later that night, Mickey vowed he'd get even and put one over on Arsenal some time in the future.

Years later, Liam Brady, who left Arsenal shortly afterwards for Juventus, put the game into perspective. 'That Cup Final will never be forgotten about simply because I don't think it will ever happen again at Wembley. I'll be very surprised if you see three goals in the last five minutes at Wembley that mean so much.'

The Racecourse Ground, January 4 1992 was an unlikely setting for any such heroics. The club's, and Mickey's, famous old Cup opponents, Arsenal, were the current First Division champions while their third-round FA Cup opponents, lowly Wrexham, had finished bottom of the fourth the previous season, only surviving the dreaded drop to non-League football because of restructuring of the part-time game. Sure the FA Cup was littered with shocks and giant-killings, but few among the Racecourse Ground crowd that chilly Saturday afternoon really believed the Welshmen would be in the hat for the Fourth Round draw come Sunday evening.

Mickey Thomas had played in bigger games, but his usual Friday night two pints of Guinness in Old Colwyn's Marine Hotel helped calm any nerves the thirty-seven-year-old might be feeling. Viewers to BBC's Football Focus were shocked to discover an aging pro recommending the benefits of the black stuff on the night before matches but Mickey reckoned, with some justification, that it made him stronger and gave him energy. The Arsenal lads, watching on their team coach as they approached Wrexham, laughed at the sight of their would-be nemesis extolling the benefits of the booze. Tony Adams and Paul Merson, both on board, knew better.

The mood in the Wrexham dressing room half an hour before kick-off was one of excitement and apprehension. Above all, the Welshmen didn't want to be on the receiving end of a thrashing. Gordon Davies paced up and down in bare feet shaking a plastic cup full of tea and stuttering: 'There's nothing to fear, lads.' It helped break the tension, but Bryan Flynn reckoned his team should simply go out and enjoy it. 'After all, ' he pointed out, 'It's eleven against eleven.'

Arsenal were the club that ruined Mickey's biggest day – the 1979 FA Cup Final – and wouldn't it be sweet revenge to send the north London giants back down the M4 with their tails between their legs? Some hope.

With eight minutes left, it looked unlikely. A typical Alan Smith strike had given Arsenal a well-deserved lead and they looked to be playing out the game when referee Kevin Breen awarded a free-kick, harshly the Arsenal bench and supporters felt, against David O'Leary for blocking Gordon Davies as the ball dropped towards the Arsenal penalty area.

Free kick, and there was only one man who was going to take it. Mickey placed the ball down, spun it until the valve faced him – the Brazilians said it gave you more power – stepped back, and the crowd behind the goal waited to watch it sail high over the bar. They'd seen Mickey score a couple from this far out but usually it was just close enough to illicit an exaggerated 'oooh' from the crowd without bothering the opposition keeper too much. This time, though, Thomas caught it just right, the ball cleared the wall and flew past Seaman's despairing dive high into the top corner to bring the Welshmen level. Mickey ran further in the next ten seconds than he had done the whole of the second half.

George Graham was furious, as was Tony Adams, but the First Division bigwigs knew another five minutes would mean an unwelcome, yet surely not over-taxing, replay at Highbury.

When Gordon Davies, the former PE teacher, wriggled free to fire a hopeful cross into the box, you'd have put your house on Tony Adams dealing safely with it. He didn't, and as the England man floundered on the floor, twenty-year-old Steve Watkin hooked the ball once more past Seaman. Pandemonium followed. Wrexham were through and Mickey had his revenge.

He also had David Seaman's gloves. Aaron Thomas, now aged eleven, was a huge fan of the England keeper and Mickey had asked before the game if the Arsenal star could spare a pair of gloves for the lad. Seaman agreed and stood in the tunnel listening to the Wrexham fans celebrating, waiting for Thomas to claim his prize. It was a great gesture and Aaron was pictured in the *Daily Express* wearing his trophy the next day.

'They were panicking,' smiled Thomas in the post-match press conference. 'Their back four just went. On their day they could have hammered us, but in the end we deserved that victory. We had everything to gain and nothing to lose. They had everything to lose – and they lost it.

'I like to think I didn't look any older than any of the lads out there today, I certainly didn't feel it. It's down to the Guinness. A couple of pints every night before a match works wonders. I've always kept myself fit and a lot of players younger than me will have trouble keeping up with me in any kind of race or training. That's why I know I can handle myself if we face West Ham (their likely Fourth Round opponents).

'I've scored some cracking goals, including a thirty-yarder against Liverpool, but this has to be the most crucial of them all and as soon as I hit it I knew it was going in.'

A shattered Mickey had cause to thank his young team-mate for snatching the winner. It saved his old bones from the ignominy of being chaired around the pitch, something Steve Watkin would never forget.

'It's the best day of my life,' he beamed. 'Eight members of my family were here to see it. It's also the best goal I've ever scored. Tony Adams mis-kicked Gordon Davies' cross and I just turned and hit it.'

Thomas and his team mates prepared to meet Farnborough Town or, more likely, West Ham, in the next round. It's a measure of Thomas' legendary status at the Racecourse that the fans have quite happily elevated Mickey's equaliser to the status of winning goal. Most of them remember that strike as the goal that sent them through. That's the Thomas magic.

Mickey couldn't wait for the Fourth Round. He always scored against West Ham.

Ten days later, he was back in the headlines. Only this time it wasn't a scorching free-kick, not even a transfer or another row with Debbie. He was charged at Deeside police station with distributing counterfeit £10 notes.

A Wrexham apprentice out for his usual Saturday evening

had tried to spend one inside the Tivoli club in Buckley, near Chester, and the police were called. They had alerted pubs and clubs throughout the area that counterfeit £10 and £20 notes were in circulation in North Wales and superintendent Brian Evans of Wrexham Police acted quickly. While police interrupted the Thomas family's Sunday lunch in Mochdre, Wrexham managing director David Rhodes was driven forty miles to the club where he let police into the dressing rooms for a search of the players' lockers. Nothing was found and directors and management of the club were not involved in the investigations.

Mickey, dressed in a blue track suit, spent two nights in the cells before being bailed for six weeks. Wrexham chairman Pryce Griffiths visited him and Liverpool star Ian Rush also phoned with words of encouragement. A thirty-minute hearing was told Thomas had allegedly supplied twenty-five dud £10 notes to an apprentice at the club, but Mickey denied all charges. His passport was taken away and he was ordered to report to Wrexham police twice a week.

West Ham duly won their FA Cup replay against non-League Farnborough, but Wrexham's Fourth Round tie at Upton Park – the ground that Mickey's brother had walked out on as a homesick trialist – seemed a long way off as Thomas rejoined his teammates at Lincoln's Sincil Bank for his first game back in the side.

It was a condition of his bail that he train away from the rest of the Wrexham team and he'd been pounding the beach at Colwyn Bay all week, turning recent events over and over in his mind. When the weather was bad he'd make do with a local leisure centre and the inevitable quips from the staff whenever he produced a note from his wallet.

'Even now if I pay for something in a shop or club, the person behind the till always makes a big deal about holding the note up to the light and checking to see if it's still wet,' he laughs. 'It wasn't a problem training alone because I was used to it. Since joining Wrexham again I'd had an arrangement with Bryan Flynn to train when I wanted to and some Mondays I could hardly get out of bed for the stiffness. He knew me well enough that I wouldn't let him down. People are always going on about my escapades off the pitch, the drinking and the high jinks, but I must have been doing something right to have played more than 700 games and still be going strong at the age of thirty-seven.'

The Lincoln game ended in a dull draw – the Wrexham lads had bigger things on their minds.

'I got some playful stick from the crowd at Lincoln,' recalls Thomas. 'But it was nothing to what I was expecting at Upton Park.'

He wasn't disappointed. As the Wrexham coach struggled through the rush hour traffic in East London, crawling the last few miles to West Ham's tight little Boleyn Ground, it was greeted by Hammers fans waving tenners at the faces of Wrexham's youngsters. They'd even had fake ones made up with Mickey's face on them. Mickey kept his head down, playing cards at the back of the bus. 'I expected to be the most hated player they'd seen there for years,' he admits. 'I knew I'd get the kind of flak I'd never had in my life but I knew they couldn't break me.

Chapter 8: The Road From Mochdre To Wembley

In fact they were playing right into my hands because I just laughed at them and rose to the occasion just like I always did when they had a go at me. The Upton Park crowd never liked me because I had a history of scoring goals against them from way back in my days at Chelsea.'

Mickey wasn't disappointed. Hate's probably too strong a word for it, the West Ham fans merely liked the fact that their no-hope visitors had someone famous they could get their teeth into. He was probably the most famous man in the ground that night. David Essex was in concert in Guildford.

Mickey led his mostly young team out wearing their change strip of yellow and green. It was exactly the same eleven who had vanquished mighty Arsenal: O'Keefe, Thackeray, Hardy, Carey, Thomas, Sertori, Davies, Owen, Connolly, Watkin and Phillips. An impossibly young looking eighteen-year-old called Lee Jones was on the bench.

Veteran Welsh striker Gordon Davies nearly didn't make it at all. He was taken ill on the morning that the team bus left Wrexham and had to make his own way to East London when he felt fit to travel. Mickey was wearing the number five shirt and was given the freedom to play where he felt he'd be most influential by Brian Flynn.

Wrexham set about their task as though West Ham should fear them. Connolly sneaked in behind Steve Potts after five minutes, a warning to the Hammers. Connolly was a typical young Wrexham player. Signed from Liverpool Sunday League team, Napoli, he'd run all day – or night as in this case.

Mickey got the bird following his first tackle. He flashed a huge grin to the crowd – it was nice to know he was still a star worthy of such attention – but that was the beginning and end of the show acting. He knew he didn't have too many nights like this left in the game and with West Ham going through a rocky patch themselves, well, you never knew what might happen in the FA Cup. Hammers fans comforted themselves with the thought that Wrexham hadn't won away from the Racecourse in fifteen months.

Mickey was involved in everything. He pinged those left-footed passes around the pitch, took the throw-ins and free-kicks, and ran and tackled as if his life depended on it. West Ham looked to have the class on their side with Slater and Keen, in particular, outstanding in the first half, but Wrexham were slowly getting on top. Gordon Davies looked very lively for an old man who'd climbed off his sick bed to be here, and the young kids in the side didn't seem overawed. Everything was going well until West Ham got a corner on the right after four-teen minutes following a sizzling free kick by Keen. It was swung in and met around the penalty spot by an unmarked Julian Dicks whose free header nestled in the bottom corner. 1-0.

Wrexham held on and the biggest cheer of the night went to Tim Breacker when he caught Mickey in possession. Mickey decided to show the crowd he still had a trick up his sleeve. A free kick outside the box had the pundits recalling the Arsenal goal and as Mickey began a long run up, the West Ham faithful broke into a chorus of whistles. Instead of blasting it as expected, Mickey stabbed his toe under the ball and dinked it just beyond the defenders to land in the space behind them. It was a brilliant idea but not even his own team mates could believe he wasn't going to shoot for goal and the chance was wasted.

Next he broke into the box, nutmegged the defender and drove a cross shot inches beyond Davies' despairing lunge. The crowd realised they had a game on their hands here. West Ham's defence was allowing Wrexham far too much time and space but at the other end McAvennie came close with a snapshot and a looping follow-up that was cleared off the line as Mitchell Thomas bore down on the goal.

Half time, 1-0 down and Wrexham were relatively happy. Brian Flynn encouraged his players to relax, take their time and look up more. They had a couple of half chances as the second half wore on but then on sixty-one minutes they got the break they deserved. A superb move led to a shot from outside the box which was deflected in front of Phillips. Potts was still favourite to clear the danger, but the Wrexham youngster somehow wrapped his right foot around the ball and sent it crashing past Miklosko in the Hammers' goal.

West Ham were clearly rattled. Slater and Keen had faded from the game and the Londoners' only hope of scoring looked like another set-piece. And so it proved when Trevor Morley glanced a header from a corner past the stranded O'Keefe who should have let his defenders deal with the danger. This was exciting, classic FA Cup fare.

Five minutes later, teenager, Lee Jones joined the fray. Steve Watkin, the real hero of the Arsenal game, brought a magnificent double save from the keeper when it looked odds on he'd score following a glorious cross-field pass from Thackeray. West Ham failed to heed the warning and moments later the same ball came popping out of the right-back position. This time Lee Jones latched on to it, out paced Breacker and, with Miklosko anticipating the shot, rolled the ball gently under the big keeper's body. The Wrexham fans corralled in the corner behind the goal went bonkers. 2-2 and another Arsenal on the cards, surely.

It almost happened too. With time running out, a blocked clearance just outside the edge of the West Ham penalty area fell like a stone a few feet in front of Mickey Thomas. He didn't wait for it to bounce but instead hit the sweetest of volleys goalward. Unfortunately Colin Foster caught the full impact of the shot and Ludo never even saw it.

At the final whistle it was as if the kids had won it for Wrexham. They lined up for press photos, stood grinning like idiots in front of the pocket of visiting supporters crammed into one corner and fell over each other to get in on the SKY TV interview from pitchside. Mickey went first.

'Unbelievable,' was his verdict. 'The lads showed great character out there after being a goal down and I thought we deserved the result in the end. Especially with ones so young in the team. Coming on the back of the Arsenal result, hopefully now we can finish them off when we get them back to Wrexham.'

He had special praise for Lee Jones. 'He's only eighteen, I'm old enough to be his dad. He took the goal ever so well and I'm so excited for him and especially the fans who travelled up here today. Wayne Phillips took his goal early, it was a great strike. He'll be thinking about that for the rest of the season, our Wayne. Tremendous.'

For his part, Phillips had no doubts as to the outcome of the replay. 'We've shown we can do it against First Division clubs with Arsenal. We've got what we wanted tonight. Get them back down to Wales and we'll beat them!'

Ten days later the two sides met in front of 20,000 fans at the Racecourse. Gordon Davies was proving his loyalty to the club once more. Ill before the last match, he'd now moved to Norway as player/coach for Tornado, but it didn't stop him heading for Wrexham when the call came. He wasn't to prove as influential this time around, but he might have if West Ham had been reduced to ten men in the first half as they should have been.

When Tim Breacker was done for pace by young Connolly it seemed the Wrexham striker would carry the ball another ten yards and let fly. He never got the chance. Breacker's clumsy lunge was never going to win the ball but he made sure his opponent ended up face down in the mud. It had to be a sending-off offence, Breacker was going to be red carded. Amazingly he escaped with a yellow, the referee later explaining that in his opinion other West Ham defenders would have barred the way to a clean run on goal. Nonsense. Wrexham were robbed of a clear goal-scoring opportunity and of justice for the offence.

Mickey, of course, lined up behind the ball just as he had against Arsenal. Another mighty run up and he dinked it cleverly over the wall again into Owen's path. This time Owen was alive to the possibility but he scuffed his shot and the danger passed. It seemed inconceivable that the First Division defence hadn't allowed for a repeat performance of Thomas' plan B free-kick, but they got away with it.

Just before the half hour West Ham won their first corner. As it swung in from the left, O'Keefe left his line and attempted to cut it out. Once more his judgement was out and Foster's soft header dropped gently into the back of the net. Three corners had now lead to three West Ham goals in this tie. The game was effectively over. West Ham dug in and put in a gritty, if unimaginative performance, while Wrexham, for all Mickey's energy and undoubted commitment, simply couldn't mount an assault on Miklosko's goal. The dream was over. It was a long second half, but the score never looked like changing. No Wrexham players volunteered for TV interviews after this one.

England and West Ham legend Bobby Moore was watching the game and he summed it up perfectly.

'Wrexham needed a little spark to lift them in the second half and they never really hurt West Ham at all. They never really lifted their performance and from Wrexham's point of view it was a disappointing second half. But full marks to them. Their performances in the FA Cup have been absolutely wonderful but they needed that little break or a little sparkle from maybe one individual to give the whole team a lift. You sensed they were having to battle against the odds all night long.'

Mickey had provided that spark to some extent. He was by far Wrexham's best player and arguably the best man on the pitch, but it's hard for thirty-seven-year-old legs to keep ploughing through a heavy pitch in a Cup replay against fitter, younger players.

'You sensed that the longer the game went on, it wasn't going to happen for them,' said Moore. 'And I think they sensed it themselves. In the Arsenal game they were still driving forward in the last ten minutes and got a result and rescued the game. They came from behind twice at Upton Park but tonight West Ham had control of the situation and it wasn't going to be Wrexham's night.'

Mickey's FA Cup heroics were over. Arsenal, Newcastle, West Ham, Tottenham and Liverpool were all there among his famous scalps. It wasn't a bad collection. West Ham v Wrexham was his fifty-fifth FA Cup tie.

9: Enter The Dragon

Mickey Thomas once said he didn't know which meant more to him, playing for Wales or playing for Manchester United. It's not something you'd hear from the mouth of Ryan Giggs. Mickey was proud of his roots, he never left them really, and his fifty-one full international caps are a testament to his commitment to the Welsh national team and the team's commitment to his talents. And yet, despite playing in Welsh teams that boasted some brilliant and internationally experienced players such as Ian Rush and Mark Hughes, he would never grace the finals of an international tournament. The Welsh hadn't reached the later stages of a major competition since the World Cup in 1958. At least that meant he didn't have to fly too often, or worry about the food – do they serve cornflakes in Spain, Italy, Mexico or Germany? But playing for Wales, particularly once he had become an established First Division star, enabled him to play with a confidence and a freedom that he was only to enjoy at club football in the twilight of his career.

Chapter 9: Enter The Dragon

Such was his importance in manager Mike England's plans that Mickey had just one period of his international career when he was in real competition for his place. Having initially been accommodated in the team alongside Derby County star, Leighton James, it soon became apparent that they were chasing the same shirt. He stepped out at Cardiff for his debut against West Germany on October 6 1976, a game in which his roasting of the experienced Bertie Vogts put him on the shopping list at Manchester United, but ended up on the losing side both here and in Glasgow a month later.

Along with Wrexham team mate Arfon Griffiths, Mickey was dropped from the starting line-up for the Racecourse clash with Czechoslovakia on March 30 the following year, but the disappointment of the home supporters, and criticism of the manager, was tempered by the 3-0 scoreline in Welsh favour. Mickey did get on, as a late replacement for Leighton James, but by then the Derby man had already scored twice.

Mickey was now James' steady substitute and he had to wait patiently for his eighth cap – a 'friendly' in Tehran – before he was on a winning side. It seemed that when James was left out, Wales missed something.

The Home Internationals, or British Championship, was a regular season's end in the late 70s and it brought much-needed cash to the coffers of the Welsh FA. Mickey played the whole match against England in Cardiff on May 13 1978, but was on the losing side again and missed the matches against Scotland and Northern Ireland. What he needed was a nice easy international match – they still had them in the 70s – to get his teeth into. Preferably at Wrexham. With a move to Manchester United being finalised he got just that when Malta came to town for an important European Championship qualifier in October. Wales won 7-0 and Mickey got his first international goal.

It gave him the confidence to express himself at the Wales training ground – he claimed nobody knew a Wrexham player when he turned up, though regular keeper, Dai Davies, was now a Wrexham man too. Mickey's game relied on confidence and controlling his nerves, and he was beginning to master both in a Welsh shirt.

By now Wales were in the swing of qualification matches and Mickey again lost to West Germany on home soil. He was excused the Home Internationals following Manchester United's FA Cup Final defeat in 1979 and returned as a substitute in Valletta to face Malta in June. Wales won again, 2-0. Leighton James was now, seemingly, out of the picture.

Mickey was sub again when the Welsh travelled, more in hope than anything else, of beating West Germany, to Cologne in October. They lost this qualifier 5-1 but the German star, Stieleke, named Mickey as the player the West Germans rated most highly in the squad. He came on to replace John Toshack, but the damage was already done. England visited Wrexham in May 1980 and with the English making noises about the tiresome Home Internationals being scrapped, the Welsh ran riot, winning 4-1 with Mickey notching another. They lost to Scotland four days later and Northern Ireland two days after that and then prepared for an opening World Cup qualifier in Iceland.

In Reykjavik, the posters advertising the game even featured Mickey's picture, so it was a surprise to everyone when his club antics seemed to spill over to his international career and he went AWOL. His son Aaron had just been born after a difficult labour for wife Debbie, and Mickey was under great pressure to stop playing football for once and look after his family.

Mickey claimed he was laid low by a 'stomach upset' and was certainly nowhere to be seen at the team's Maidenhead training ground. But he was still due to meet up with the rest of the squad at Heathrow airport and when he didn't show, manager Mike England claimed he was baffled as to Mickey's whereabouts. It meant a second cap for Mickey's old mate Gordon Davies and as a result Thomas was dropped by Mike England and missed three of the next four internationals. He was recalled a year later when he helped overcome Scotland at Swansea, draw 0-0 with England at Wembley and grind out the same result against the USSR in a World Cup qualifier at the Racecourse ground on May 30 1981.

He was in and out of the side again now, his nomadic club reputation taking its toll and was often subbed or sitting on the bench as the Welsh World Cup campaign began to fizzle out. This was a crucial period for the Welsh. From being favourites of all five British Isles nations to qualify, they were now rank out-siders as they prepared to travel to Tblisi to meet the Russians once more.

'Maybe that suits us,' reckoned Welsh skipper and future Wrexham boss, Brian Flynn. 'Now perhaps we can get back to playing our best football. Suddenly we are underdogs and the pressure is off. That's the way it was when we started: then we had four straight wins against Iceland, Turkey twice and Czecho-slovakia. When we drew 0-0 against the Russians at Wrexham, it was nine points out of ten and not a goal scored against us.'

From then on nothing had gone right for Wales. They lost 2-0 in Czechoslovakia and were left speechless when the impos-sible happened and Iceland drew 2-2 at the Vetch Field when Mike England picked six Swansea players on their own pitch.

'We have to win in Tblisi,' said Flynn. 'Our position in Group Three is very straightforward; two points or it's all over. No one believes that we will reach Spain and that means we can relax instead of being so uptight.'

Mike England was furious with his forwards for missing so many chances in the Iceland draw. But there still wasn't a role for Mickey.

'Chances were tossed away against Iceland,' he fumed. 'If we hadn't created them in the first place, then I would have been worried. But we did create them, it was simply that they were not taken. There has to be a huge improvement against the Russians.'

It never materialised. The Russians strolled to a 3-0 victory and it was all over.

It was difficult to pick Mickey for the international squad when he spent most of his time at Brighton, missing, but his eventual move to Stoke City coincided with the start of another European Championship campaign and with his best form for some time. He has featured as a substitute on an embarrassing night in May when Wales entertained Northern Ireland at the Racecourse. The game went into the record books as the lowest gate for an international match in Great Britain with just 2,315 Wrexham punters bothering to turn out. Mickey was recalled for the 1-0 win over Norway on September 22 1982, played his part in a thrilling 4-4 draw against Yugoslavia in Titograd a week before Christmas and in a 1-0 Racecourse ground victory over Bulgaria on April 27 1983. Only England at Wembley had spoiled the party with a 2-1 win in February. Brazil came to Cardiff on June 12 1983 and Mickey revelled in the carnival atmosphere – yes, even in Cardiff – and the chance to try some of his tricks against the masters. A 1-1 draw, courtesy of Brian Flynn's goal, was a great result. They drew a European Championship qualifier 0-0 in September, stuffed Romania 5-0 a month later at Wrexham – Mickey got another – and then prepared to face Bulgaria in Sofia for a vital European Qualifier.

Wales could virtually book their place at the Finals in France with a win in Sofia. But pundits urged Mike England to go for the draw and then clinch qualification with a draw at home to Yugoslavia. Gordon Davies, who would team up with Mickey at Chelsea and Wrexham, had other ideas.

'Let's be bold and snatch that place here and now,' he urged. 'It could all depend on whether the boss is bold enough to go all out for that win in Sofia. I could well understand if he was more cautious. It might be that the other results will work out to our benefit so that we might have qualified by the time the Yugoslavs come to Wales next month.

'Either way it's a big thing for the nation. It would be a great thrill to reach the Finals and to be ranked among the top eight in Europe, especially after the disappointment of missing out on the World Cup Finals.'

The Welsh played it cautious. Ian Rush cut a lonely figure up front with Mickey Thomas working hard on the left of midfield to supply him. It didn't pay off and the Bulgarians scored the only goal of the game. Wales duly secured the draw against Yugoslavia at Ninian Park in December, but, after the disappointment in Sofia, it wasn't good enough for qualification.

Now at Chelsea and getting used to winning again, Mickey played in the 1-0 victory over England at Wrexham on May 2 1984 but missed the trip to Norway and Israel a month later. Another World Cup qualifying group, this time for the right to play in the Finals in Mexico, was upon the Welsh and this time Mickey made it to Iceland for a 1-0 defeat on September 12. He was substituted in Valencia a month later as Spain won comfortably 3-0 but scored, along with Mark Hughes, against Iceland when they came to Cardiff in November.

Things were getting serious now and the Welsh travelled to Glasgow for a crunch World Cup qualifier in March 1985. If they lost to Scotland their World Cup dream would be shattered. Up front, Mark Hughes and Ian Rush were forging an impressive strike force, fed by Mickey and Peter Nicholas. The Welsh reckoned they might just nick it, and Mickey's money was on 'Sparky' Hughes to hit the mark.

'He's one of the sharpest strikers in Britain,' said Mickey. 'He's fast and strong with a tremendous finish that stems from his first touch. Mark can kill a ball stone dead in a melee of defenders and this buys him time where other forwards need a second stab to get the ball under control. With him and Rushie in the forward line we've got the pace to take on Alex McLeish and Willie Miller and the finishing power to beat Jim Leighton.'

As it turned out, Ian Rush scored the only goal to keep the dream alive. He and Hughes were on the score sheet again for a brilliant 3-0 win over Spain at Wrexham, and now all eyes turned to the Scotland game in Cardiff on September 10. Mickey was on his way out of Chelsea at the time. A broken jaw in pre-season and the arrival of Micky Hazard had convinced him it was time for another move, but Mike England kept faith with him that night. It was to become one of the most extraordinary and most talked about games the two countries would ever play.

The crowds walking up to Ninian Park were buzzing with anticipation, Welsh and Scots indulging in their favourite battle hymn – 'If you all hate the English clap your hands.' Those few of us present in the throng who were English kept our heads down. The mathematics were simple. Wales needed to win to qualify for Mexico, Scotland simply needed to avoid defeat to be sure, at least, of a play-off place against Oceania Group winners, Australia. 39,500 nervous souls were packed into the ground. Even the neutrals couldn't help but be caught up in the drama of it all.

Wales set off like men possessed and Scotland prepared to weather the storm. They'd been doing so for thirteen minutes when a half fit Peter Nicholas came out of a challenge with two Scottish defenders with the ball at his feet. He surged into the box, got to the byline and pulled back a cross that was met by Mark Hughes who coolly slipped it past a distinctly uncomfort-able looking Jim Leighton. 1-0, the place went mad. But

Scotland gradually found their feet and while goalmouth excitement was hard to find, the atmosphere in the stadium was electric.

Jim Leighton never reappeared after the break but the Welsh didn't really provide his replacement, Alan Rough, with too many problems. Rush did take one uncharacteristic swing at a Hughes cross shot but he missed the ball completely and the Scots rallied. Considering they were making do without Dalglish (injured) and Souness (suspended) they were doing well. Davie Cooper came on for Strachan, after Nicoll refused to notice the number seven waved virtually under his nose, with thirty minutes left on the clock. His introduction proved decisive. Cooper began running at the heart of the tiring Welsh defence and was causing problems. A deep cross from Nicoll was headed down by Sharp and the ball struck Phillips's hand as he battled with David Speedie, Mickey's Chelsea team mate. Referee Keizer pointed to the spot.

The Welsh couldn't believe it. In 1978 they had been knocked out in similarly controversial circumstances by the Scots when a penalty was given against them when the Scottish striker, Joe Jordan, then Mickey's Manchester United team mate, handled the ball in the Welsh area. Don Masson put that one away to send the Scots to Argentina and eliminate Wales. Now it was happening all over again. Southall got two hands to Cooper's spot kick but it was too powerful and the Scots had their late equaliser. There were still ten minutes left to play but the Scots weren't going to take any chances now.

Would Wales ever make it to a World Cup Finals? They'd

taken three points off Scotland, rattled in three goals against Spain on another memorable evening and in Mark Hughes and Ian Rush they now possessed two of the hottest strikers in international football.

But the drama wasn't over yet. As the final whistle blew, a melee of photographers massed around the Scottish dugout. Something was wrong. Stewards were clearing people out of the way, but most of the crowd were oblivious to the drama unfolding on the edge of the pitch. Jock Stein, legendary Scottish team boss and former Celtic supremo, had lurched forward at the sound of the final whistle, the victim of a massive heart attack. Stein was rushed to hospital as fast as they could get an ambulance through the singing and dancing Scots fans outside, but it didn't look good.

Back at the team hotel an hour later, Mickey Thomas was trying to hide the sadness and disappointment of the night. He was dishing out bottles of champagne to anyone and everyone when Mike England walked in looking pale and shocked. The Wales boss confirmed the sad news. Stein was dead. The party was over and the few Scottish supporters able to afford such luxurious billets sat stony-faced and drank a toast to the most famous man in Scottish football.

Jock Stein had done more for Scottish football in twenty years than anyone in the history of the game, north of the border. He was the classic Scottish footballing man – born in a mining village and working down the pits in Lanarkshire into his mid twenties. He didn't beat about the bush and he didn't suffer fools gladly. In 1967 his Celtic side lifted the European

Cup – the first British side to do so – after defeating Internazionale of Milan in Lisbon. In thirteen years as manager of Celtic his side won ten championships, including the now equalled nine in a row. He wasn't the greatest player, but his determination and will to succeed made him a perfect acquisition for Celtic at a time when they were looking for someone to not only join the playing staff, but coach the youngsters as well. He left Celtic Park in 1978 for Leeds United but was soon back in Scotland as manager of a national side in desperate need of a restoration of pride after the humiliation of the Argentine World Cup. He had suffered a mild heart attack in 1977, but the shock in Cardiff, and the footballing world in general, at the loss of a great footballing man, was palpable that evening.

Welsh football had its heart broken too that night. Joey Jones, Mickey's greatest mate and veteran of the previous Scotland controversy, just wandered around muttering to nobody in particular, 'Well, that's my last chance gone. Finished. I can't believe they've done us again with a dodgy penalty.' Scotland went on to beat Australia and make it to the Finals. Wales had missed out by a point.

An unwelcome Ninian Park match against Hungary loomed the following month, and Mickey, now a West Bromwich Albion player, turned out. The Welsh hearts still hadn't mended and they lost 3-0. Saudi Arabia in February 1985 at least held the promise of a bit of sun and Mickey boarded the plane and set off to sit on the sub's bench. He did get on – in place of Clayton Blackmore after sixty two minutes, but that would be his last international. He went out on a 2-1 away win.

MICKEY THOMAS' WELSH CAPS

1976: v W. Germany, Scotland. 1977: Czechoslovakia (plus 1 as sub), Scotland (plus 1 as sub), N.Ireland (sub), Kuwait (sub). 1978: v Iran, England, N. Ireland (sub), Malta, Turkey. 1979: v West Germany (plus 1 as sub), Malta (sub), Rep of Ireland, Turkey. 1980: v England, Scotland, N.Ireland, Czechoslovakia. 1981: v Scotland, England, USSR (plus 1 as sub) , Czechoslovakia. 1982: v Spain, England, Scotland (sub), N. Ireland (sub), Norway, Yugoslavia. 1983: v England, Bulgaria (twice), Scotland, N. Ireland, Brazil, Romania, Yugoslavia. 1984: Scotland, England, Iceland (twice), Spain. 1985: Scotland (twice), Spain, Norway, Hungary, Saudi Arabia (sub).

Total appearances: 51. Goals: 4 v Malta ('78), England ('80), Romania ('83), Iceland ('84).

10: A Stab In The Dark

Mickey Thomas wasn't the first professional footballer to have sex with another man's wife and it's a fair bet he won't be the last. While perhaps not an official part of the PFA handbook, extra-marital affairs at least give young, fit, professional sportsmen something to do with all that spare time and energy. Mickey Thomas wasn't even the first man to have sex with another man's wife in a car, but he was almost certainly the first man to be stabbed fifteen times in the backside with a screwdriver by her husband while doing it.

Barely a month after pushing his thirty-eight-year-old bones through another torturous pre-season, Mickey was in hospital having treatment to stab wounds to his left buttock, lower back and left leg, as well as a suspected fractured jaw. Not surprisingly, he wasn't fit for Wrexham's home game against Rochdale the following day.

Details of the attack were sketchy at first. Mickey had parked his Volkswagen in a country lane at Dyserth near Prestatyn,

Clwyd. Two men armed with a screwdriver and a hammer smashed the window and attacked him, leaving him semi-conscious in a pool of blood. Luckily for Mickey, a passing motorist stopped to investigate what looked like an abandoned vehicle and took the injured star to hospital in nearby St Asaph where he was released after treatment.

Back home in Colwyn Bay, Mickey's solicitor, Don Roberts, was answering the phone. 'Mickey is not very well and his family is very distressed,' he told reporters. 'I'm not prepared or able to give any names of the people involved. They are being sought by the police and neither I nor Mickey want to jeopardise the inquiry.'

Mickey's passenger in the car, a twenty-nine-year-old woman, was interviewed by detectives before being released without charge but it was clear that something strange had occurred. Why would two men, apparently stumbling on a couple down a well-known lover's lane, decided to viciously attack one occupant of the vehicle? It was a question Mickey was asking himself.

Four days later it seemed the police had the answer. Mickey's former brother-in-law, thirty-two-year-old Geoffrey Dean, was accused of attempted murder and remanded by Prestatyn magistrates. Dean protested his innocence, but it left some intriguing questions unanswered. Was Thomas set up or was he merely followed by an enraged husband who just happened to be his former wife's brother? This, of course, meant the woman in the car was Mickey's sister-in-law. The questions remained unanswered for almost a year.

'Love Romp Attackers Are Jailed' screamed the headlines of

the *North Wales Weekly News* as Mickey's assailants were finally
made to pay for the cowardly attack of almost a year before.

'Two men who attacked soccer star Mickey Thomas of
Mochdre as he was indulging in a love romp in a secluded lane
have been jailed for three years,' the paper reported on July 22
1993. 'One of the men's wives had been used as 'bait' to attract
former Welsh international and Manchester United ace, Mr
Thomas, to the lonely spot after the men decided on a revenge
attack. His former brother-in-law, Geoffrey Dean, 33, and busi-
nessman Mark Gorovan, 27, both admitted unlawfully wounding Mr Thomas last August. Geoffrey's wife, Erica, 30, also
admitted unlawfully wounding Thomas, who was her childhood
sweetheart before she married Geoffrey in 1981. Mr Thomas
married Geoffrey's sister, Debbie, the mother of his two
children.'

Prosecuting counsel, Michael Farmer, told the court that the
previous year, Erica and Geoffrey Dean's marriage had started to
have difficulties and that she had resumed her affair with her
famous ex-boyfriend, meeting. him a number of times and
making love in his car. However, Mr Farmer claimed, the
meeting on August 20 had been engineered by Geoffrey Dean to
put Thomas in a vulnerable position and give him an opportunity to beat him up. If so, it worked a treat. Farmer told a hushed
courtroom that as Mickey and Erica made love, parked in a lane
between St Asaph and Dyserth, the car's window was smashed in
and Thomas was then punched in the face.

His assailants didn't plan their attack too meticulously or set
about covering their tracks too expertly. According to Mickey's

evidence, as the blows rained down on him he heard a voice shout 'Run, Erica, run!' so he knew it wasn't an opportunist attack by persons unknown. He was then attacked with a hammer and a screwdriver while Gorovan threatened to cut his ear and penis off, break his legs and scar his face. Mickey later told friends that his attackers had literally added insult to injury. When, as he slipped in and out of consciousness, he heard one voice say 'Cut his dick off!' The other had replied 'We'll have to find it first!'

Judge Elgan Edwards sentenced the two men, both from Rhyl, to two years each for the attack on Mickey plus a further one year each for an earlier bully-boy attack on a Rhyl night-clubber the previous April. Sexual bait, Erica, fared better. Now pregnant, the Judge explained he would be more lenient on her because of her condition. He believed she had been forced into the act by her husband and that she, at least, had shown real con-trition. She was ordered to do 180 hours community service – valeting cars perhaps – as the judge said he had no desire to see her child born in prison and thereby deprive her children of both of their parents.

Despite the overwhelming weight of prosecution evidence, defending counsel Marc Leon had tried his best.

'One can imagine what was effectively going through his [Dean's] mind when he knew his wife was committing adultery with someone who had ruined the marriage of his sister,' he told the court as he described how Dean's marriage was at a low point.

Erica Dean was branded 'shameful' for her part in the affair.

Mickey was as upbeat, if slightly stiffer, as ever. 'I'll tell you this much, it certainly changed my attitude to safe sex,' he claimed later. 'Now if a girl asks whether I've taken precautions, I say, 'Yeah, I've locked the doors and hidden the tool kit!'

It was a weight off his mind, but no sooner had Mickey endured one court case than another loomed rapidly on the horizon. Returning home from Chester Crown Court, a look at the calendar confirmed he had one week before Warrington Crown Court would consider the matter of the dud £10 notes.

Mickey couldn't help but wonder whether the next trial would have a very different outcome. Never a great sleeper, even when things were going well, he sat at home in Mochdre watching his videos, turning things over and over in his mind. And yet playing football hadn't been put to the back of his brain. He still had enough enthusiasm, and talent, to be much in demand in Welsh football. He'd officially retired when he left Wrexham in May but was now keeping in shape training with Konica League of Wales side, Conwy United, and, according to those who knew him, looking forward to challenging for a regular place in the side.

The local papers sensationally revealed that after a successful Tuesday night training session Mickey would pull on his boots for Conwy and face a star-studded Oldham Athletic side in a pre-season friendly at the club's Morfa ground barely a week before the trial.

Manager Mark Jones confirmed: 'Mickey will definitely be guesting for us on Saturday and I'm very hopeful he will sign forms in the next week. I know his situation at the moment is a bit delicate, but I regard it as quite a coup for the club and I believe he could still do a tremendous job for us once he becomes available.'

Conwy weren't the only club keeping an eye on Mickey's availability. But United could count on family connections – his son Aaron had also played for the Conwy Borough Junior side – and Conwy's manager was in no doubt that his new star's presence would boost the gate against Oldham.

'Oldham have done us proud in naming a very strong squad and with Mickey playing for us it's a match that should attract a really good crowd.'

When Saturday came around, Mickey found himself more nervous than he would have thought possible. Maybe it was the fear that this might be his last game of football as a free man, or the fact that Oldham were evidently taking the game very seriously, naming the likes of Ian Marshall in their forward line. Whatever it was, Mickey went through his pre-match ritual of putting his boots on three times, much to the amusement of the part-time players sitting half-changed around him. He struggled to make a mark and found it tough going, particularly in a first half that saw Oldham take the lead after just five minutes when Conwy's guest star lost possession. Whoops!

But as the game wore on the crowd of just 400 were at last treated to some of the old Thomas magic. One thunderous free kick, reminiscent of his finest moment in a Wrexham shirt, was tipped over the bar by the Latics' keeper and Mickey watched hopefully as a couple of shots flew wide of the post in the second half. In the end, Oldham ran out comfortable 3-0 winners.

After the match Mickey tried to put the next few weeks out of his mind and concentrate on his football. 'It was very hard but I enjoyed it,' he told local journalists. 'I've obviously had a lot on my mind in the past few weeks and it was nice to have the chance to have a game of football and forget about everything for a while. I started my career here with Conwy Juniors and it would be nice to finish it here, but we have to wait and see what the next few weeks hold in store. Football is still my first love and I'd like to carry on playing if my legs will let me and hopefully that will be with Conwy.

'They have been very kind to me. I am forty next year but I look after myself. I eat the right things and don't put on much weight – I'd like to think I've got a couple of more seasons left in me, given the chance. I've played football all over the world at the top level and I'd like to pass on some of that experience to the kids.'

It sounded like an early plea for clemency from the trial judge.

When the big day finally came, Mickey's lawyer was to be found in magnificent full flow, pleading on behalf of his client; 'He is a foolish man,' he told the court. 'His judgement is at its best on the field not in his private affairs.'

But it was an open and shut case. It emerged that some Wrexham youngsters paid around £5 each for the fake tenners and that Thomas had managed to offload around £840 worth of the notes between November 1991 and January 1992 – the same time as he was scoring that famous goal and knocking Arsenal out of the FA Cup. Along with co-defendant Alex Roache, Mickey was sentenced to eighteen months as he laughed and waved at Joey Jones and other mates in the courtroom. Judge Gareth Edwards was not amused.

'You should have been setting young apprentices an example of how a true professional conducts himself,' he chastised Thomas. 'Instead, largely I think because it fitted in with your self-image of a flash and daring adventurer, you betrayed the trust of your employers. And you failed in your duty as a distinguished international sportsman. I do not see how you can possibly escape prison for offences such as these.'

As Mickey was led away he quipped 'Anyone got change for £10 for the phone?'

Outside the courtroom, the Thomas family were understandably shocked. Mickey wasn't a bad lad, they reasoned, a bit lacking in judgement at times perhaps but not the criminal type. They couldn't believe he'd been locked up. It seemed to them he'd already served twelve months with the trial hanging over him and now it felt like there had been a death in the family. Phil Thomas blamed his brother's Jack-the-lad image for landing him in hot water once too often. But, he claimed, it was an image his brother didn't deserve and one that couldn't be further from the truth.

'He's so different to what people imagine,' he explained. 'I've been all over the world with him and he's always been the same. When he was playing for Chelsea, Manchester United and Everton, people would assume he'd be out on the town after a match but the truth was he'd get showered, change, get in his car and drive 250 miles home to Mochdre to be with his mum and kids. Even playing at Wrexham he still had that playboy image and he was always back home by eight and would spend the weekend with his kids, and ours, playing cards and video games.'

Phil was the first visitor to Kirkham to check on his brother and was with him when he was taken down to the cells joking and waving to his mates in court. 'I was with him after the trial and I could tell he was shaken up by it,' said Phil. 'Even though he tried not to show it. He was totally dumbfounded and I know he was sat there wondering why he was there.'

Mickey wasn't short of good character references at the trial. His old school, St Joseph's, wrote to the court as did Ysgol Pen Y Bryn, and many other local people from Mochdre and Colwyn Bay.

'He cares about his home town and the people in it,' continued Phil. 'Money has never meant that much to him.'

The pressure on the Thomas family as a whole had begun to tell with Phil, Mum Maureen, eldest brother Kevin and sister Pauline all having to change their phone numbers because of constant calls from the Sunday papers in London. Mickey's mum was hit hardest. She stayed indoors watching the piles of videos of her son's greatest matches, devastated by his sentence.

'The phones never stopped ringing,' said Phil. 'But I never bothered with the press, television or radio until now.'

You could hardly blame Fleet Street for its voracious interest. A footballer, an unfaithful sister-in-law, a multiple stabbing with a screwdriver and a bundle of dodgy tenners was simply too good a story not to pursue with vigour – and pursue it they did. If only Erica had been a nun, then it would have been the story of the decade!

Phil was certain that his brother would get back to playing the game he loved when he was eventually released.

'He should serve around nine months of the eighteen and he was super fit when he went inside and should still be when he comes out,' he said. 'I saw him the morning of the Conwy game a couple of weeks ago and he was so excited and keyed up. Exactly the same as when he was playing for Manchester United, Wales or any big club.'

Outside the courtroom, Mickey's old sparring partner, Joey Jones, echoed the thoughts of his family.

'He can count on them and his friends for support,' said the Wrexham coach. 'They are a very strong and close-knit family and I still find it hard to believe he's been sent to prison – he just isn't the criminal type. He always lived life to the full and enjoyed a laugh and a joke but he'd give you his last penny – he's one of my best mates.'

Mickey Thomas' life was now out of his control. There was nowhere to run to, nowhere to hide. Sitting in the back of the police van delivering new inmates to Kirkham Prison, near Blackpool, Mickey suddenly realised what he faced. The man who had always had an escape route back to North Wales when the pressure got too much now faced spending twenty-three hours a day locked in his cell.

Once inside he was ordered to empty his pockets – revealing a roll of Monopoly money which he aimed to autograph for fellow inmates, much to the amusement of the prison warders – then to strip and shower, before being given his bedding and taken to his cell.

One warder asked the nervous newcomer if he had a drink or drugs problem. Mickey shook his head. 'Well you will have by the time you fucking leave here,' he roared as the cell door banged shut.

Life at Kirkham wasn't as bad as Thomas had feared. Not everyone liked the idea of a celebrity prisoner being on their landing and he had to watch his back. He was shaken one day when a prisoner began hammering his fists on the cell door accusing the new boy of getting special treatment. He wasn't.

'The only perk I got was cleaning the landing,' says Mickey. 'That meant you weren't banged up for up to twenty-three hours a day. I was locked up in my cell at about seven pm and that's it. It's bad news if your cell mate is boring – but if that's all he is you've had a result! I suppose having a screwdriver shoved in your arse is as good an introduction to sharing a cell in prison as you'll get! Luckily my cell-mate was this huge guy with a broken nose who was a devoted United fan. He told me he wouldn't let anyone touch me and thankfully he was as good as his word.'

Mickey's sentence became the focus for some old-fashioned 'lock em up and throw away the key' attacks on what was seen as a far too easy regime inside Kirkham. Coming on the back of Home Secretary Michael Howard's Tory Party conference declaration that prison shouldn't be a picnic and that Butlins need not apply to run the new privatised prisons, pictures of Thomas playing bowls and enjoying a can of lager with fellow inmates were published by the *News Of The World* in October.

Prison governor, Alf Jennings, was shocked. 'We don't allow beer or champagne inside,' he said. 'But we do have visitors who plant stuff for pick-ups by the inmates. We have a constant campaign against drink.'

Mickey had also raised eyebrows by informing his mates – via the prison telephone – that he was also enjoying a new hobby – fishing!

'The fishing pond was made from a natural pond and a sump for the playing fields,' said Governor Jennings. 'There are roach and perch in there.' Even the Home Office was brought in for comment on Mickey's life at Kirkham. 'It is unusual for your average prison,' agreed a spokesman. 'But if the fishing pond was built by inmates then that was a thoroughly constructive thing. Prisoners have association time when they socialise with each other and that's very important. But clearly alcohol isn't allowed.'

Mickey also enjoyed the occasional game of bowls and was put in charge of the prison football team's kit. The prison laundry proved a useful hideaway for the occasional can of lager.

Rent-a-quote Tory MP Geoffrey Dickens reacted predictably. 'God help us! I always thought a sentence was punishment. If a victim sees how these prisoners are treated it's twisting the knife. Many don't have that kind of luxury.' Fellow Tory, Nicholas Winterton agreed. 'People are going to say here are those who have done the crime and he's going out fishing, watching TV and living the sort of life I can't afford. And I'm the innocent party. We need a regime in prison that meets the expectation of people outside – the victims.'

Mickey may not have been chained to his bed, but he was never allowed to forget that his new 'mates' were a different breed.

'I was stuck in with the lifers for some reason,' he says. 'I remember watching TV with a bloke doing life for murder and a programme came on about a lunatic who'd been sent down for killing someone with a hammer. He turned to me and said, 'See, that's how bloody unfair it is. I only strangled mine! It's amazing but the thing I remember most was that the inmates' favourite programme was Prisoner Cell Block H. Honest.'

Not surprisingly the Kirkham authorities wasted no time in recruiting Mickey to the prison team. He was brilliant, easily able to dodge the tackles that came flying in from anyone hoping to put him in his place. He kept fit in the prison gym and even now at thirty-nine, he was too clever and quick for opposition rough-house tactics.

Not that the games, all played at 'home', were without inci-dent. While the world outside turned its attention to World Cup USA in July 1994, Kirkham prepared to face a team from the local Whitbread brewery. The game was finally abandoned after two Whitbread players were carried from the pitch and the Kirkham keeper raced the length of the pitch to head-butt a spectator who later required eight stitches to the wound.

The keeper, thirty-seven-year-old Peter Southern, was brought to Preston Crown Court to face the music where he claimed Michael Hall had hurled sexual insults at him.

Mickey couldn't keep out of it. His name was brought up and he was credited with giving the match an added significance merely due to his presence on the pitch. He had nothing to do with the incident or the brawl which followed. Southern, already serving three years for wounding, was given a further four months to run concurrently.

One of Mickey's prison team mates, now safely back watching his beloved Wrexham on a more regular basis, recalls the confines and adventures of the Kirkham First XI.

'I actually played in Mickey's football team at Kirkham,' he says. 'I was inside for fraud and the main thing I remember about it was how bloody cold it always was. We started playing in November and it was freezing. We used to play every Saturday morning on a bit of playing field and everyone took it really seriously. Mickey was working in the gym at Kirkham and he'd pick the side along with the PT instructor.

'We'd play anyone really. I remember once Blackburn Rovers reserves came down and we kicked them all over the place. I think they wished they hadn't bothered really. Having Mickey in the side always livened things up, but sometimes, if it was really freezing, he'd maybe walk off at half time and let someone else play so he could go and get out of the cold.'

The prison team was often on the end of some well-meant, but unwelcome, visits by teams of concerned professionals keen to see the inmates given the chance of some decent recreation and exercise.

'We played a team of doctors one weekend and they all turned up thinking this was a nice gesture and we'd all respect them,' says Mickey's mate. 'We kicked lumps out of them and they all walked off the pitch about half way through the second half because they couldn't believe it. We were terrible really. Maybe that's why we didn't have too many away games.

'It wasn't pleasant in there, obviously, but it wasn't too bad.

We were all professional people billeted together. You didn't find yourself sharing a cell with a murderer or a rapist or anything like that. We were all solicitors, accountants, that type of thing, and there was a famous bank manager who'd emptied the vault and done a runner with all the cash.

'Mickey was too good for that team, obviously. He was the only one who played really and he kept himself fit by working in the gym. I'm a Wrexham supporter so it's great for me to be able to say I played in the same team as Mickey Thomas.'

Perhaps partly due to the publicity generated by his perceived life-style in Kirkham, Mickey was moved to Walton, where he once more became a star of the prison team. Before long he was on the move again – this time to Sudbury prison where he would see out the remainder of the nine months he would eventually serve. If the regime at Kirkham had looked more cosy than it was, Sudbury Prison, near Derby, was a veritable haven.

'I always got on really well with the warders and inmates,' says Mickey. 'One early evening I was allowed out with a prison officer and we stopped off on the way back to Sudbury for a drink. He wanted to go sharpish but I managed to persuade him to stay for a few more. Anyway by the time we got back to the prison, we'd been locked out. We couldn't find anyone to let us in so eventually we had no alternative but to break in. Imagine if I'd got caught – the first inmate to be caught breaking into a prison!'

It sounded like a steal from a famous episode of Ronnie Barker's famous prison sitcom, *Porridge*, but if anyone could pull off such a stunt it would have to be Mickey Thomas. Sad to think his last season in professional football was thrown away for the sake of an unspectacular £840. Nine months inside – the length of the average English football season. What a waste. On his release from Sudbury, Mickey headed for the beach at Colwyn Bay. The air had never smelt so sweet.

11: 'I Felt Sick When He Left For United'

To this day you can mingle with the Wrexham fans along Mold Road before the match and spend hours talking about Mickey Thomas. Sweet talk your way past the bouncers on the door of the Turf Hotel – the 'home' pub with its balcony that looks directly out over the pitch – and they'll recall Mickey starring in European nights when the extra floodlights were allowed to be turned on, internationals coming back to the Racecourse after years of Ninian Park's dominance, and of course, the goal against Arsenal. Here then are the memories of some of those fans.

'The greatest memory has to be the goal against Arsenal in the FA Cup. I was here that day. We were written off before the game even started. We were supposed to be no-hopers, they were the Champions of England and even though we were Welsh we were still in the same league. We were bottom of the fourth division – should have perhaps been kicked out of the League – and Arsenal came up here thinking, well we're on for a nice training session here, but Mickey upset them.

'I know that before that, the era when John Neal was manager here, perhaps one of the best managers we've had here over the past thirty years, he brought through a team that included the likes of Mickey. We had the likes of Joey Jones, Bobby Shinton, Billy Ashcroft, Eddie Niedzwiecki, and that was a very, very good team.

'I've been following Wrexham since 1964 and I'd put Mickey Thomas, definitely, in the top five players we've ever had at the club. Along with the likes of Graham Whittle, whose brother Alan played at Everton, who used to play here, and was a really good player at the same time. But Mickey went from here to Manchester United and I think every other club in the country had a taste of him, and he did all right for himself.

'When he left for Manchester United I was devastated because the team broke up within one season. He wasn't the only one, there were six or seven players who went that same season and people wondered why the following season we were relegated. But I can remember Mickey playing for Wrexham against Sheffield Wednesday and we beat them 3-0 to go top of the old Second Division and from then on it was downhill all the way! But whenever he did play for Wrexham he always did do his best.'

'It was his speed, wasn't it? He was so quick. So quick and very skilful. I felt sick when he left for United but like a lot of good players we have here, they go, and you get used to it. When he came back for a second spell it brought a bit of excitement to the club again to have him back. It was good to see him and he came and did the business didn't he? He scored that goal which got us into the fifth round of the Cup. It was great. They say players shouldn't come back – and we've had several players who have come back here and shouldn't have come back, but Mickey Thomas came back, didn't he, and did the business.

'If you had a Wrexham team of all time, he'd be in it, definitely. He's got to be near the top because he made Manchester United and Everton. He played well when he was here originally and when he came back. I never saw him play for Wales because it's a long way to go down to Cardiff, but I have seen Wales play here at the Racecourse Ground. They should share it out a bit more.'

'He always gave 110% every game. He was absolutely superb and he's been a great servant to this club. His greatest moment was probably playing in the Cup Final with Manchester United, but he has said the highlight of his career was scoring that goal here against Arsenal. We've had many great players here over the year but he's up there with the best of them. He was in a superb team. The team that got promotion in 77-78 was brilliant. It was the best team the Second or Third Division will ever see.'

'When he went to Manchester United I thought 'good luck to the lad.' It goes without saying that we hate them, but good luck to him. Everybody deserves the chance to better themselves. If they get the chance, take it, without a doubt. Mind you, I must admit I was a bit annoyed when he came back the following season and said, That stand up there, I paid for that.'

'When he came back to Wrexham we were right down the bottom and Mickey did a great job helping the young players that were in that team to come through. It was a pity about the money. He did a good job.'

'He was very good really. Good midfielder and I always thought he had it in him to go on and play in the First Division, which he did eventually. It was a bit sad when he left but at the time we had a good team here. John Neal was a good manager at the time. When he came back he did well for us and he'll be living off that Arsenal goal forever. It was just a bit unfortunate in the end.'

'He was our little star really – the first time around. You could stop him and have a chat in the car park, he was never too big headed to remember the fans who paid to come and watch him. They say you should never come back but we wouldn't be challenging for promotion now if he hadn't come back and helped Brian Flynn bed in some of the youngsters at the club now.'

'I think everyone remembers him because whenever things got on top of him he would head straight back to Wales wouldn't he? There are so-called stars in the Welsh team now who can hardly be bothered to turn out for matches. Mickey was never like that – and he played for Manchester United too. I remember seeing him play here at the Racecourse against Northern Ireland in front of a couple of thousand. It was a miserable night but he ran his heart out. That was Mickey Thomas.'

'He's probably our most famous player of all time. I know he did some stupid things and got into a lot of trouble over the years but a lot of people have only ever heard of Wrexham football club because of Mickey Thomas. There aren't too many players you could say that about are there?'

Mickey Thomas

'I watched every Wales game he ever played in – in Wrexham. I've never been to Ninian Park to watch Wales, it's too far for us up here, but I'll tell you what. The reason they started bringing the internationals back here was because of Mickey Thomas. The Welsh FA knew they'd get decent crowds and that Mickey would run all night because we were all here cheering him on.'

12: "I Suppose I Just Used To Get Fed Up And Bugger Off"

I spent a weekend in Colwyn Bay, Mochdre and Wrexham talking to people about Mickey Thomas. On a beautiful May evening with the tide coming and just a few cars parked on the Prom, it was very easy to see why he could never shake this place out of his system. Walk from Colwyn Bay along to Rhys-on-Sea and you'll feel the stresses and strains of modern life falling away with every wave lapping against the sea wall. That weekend, with a minimum of detective work, it was easy to find people to talk to about their most famous resident. Everyone knew him, everyone had a story to tell about him. They love him. They love him at Chelsea and at Manchester United and Stoke too. There are Everton fans, I've met them, who don't even realise he played for the club, and you can add Leeds and Derby fans to that category. Brighton? Well they've got other things on their minds.

Mickey Thomas was a fan's player because no matter in what position the particular team he was playing at the time found itself, he always gave 110%. That's what fans want to see. They don't care if you make mistakes, as long as you take playing for their club as seriously as they do supporting it. When his final ball was letting him down in the 1979 Cup Final he didn't stop trying to play it. When the odds against little Wrexham following up their defeat of the English Champions with another Cup shock at West Ham were so short, not even Lou Macari would bet on them, Mickey called on reserves of stamina and guile to help see his side through to a replay after a storming match in East London.

And he did all that with a charm and a vulnerability that was probably a vital part of his survival kit as a little kid on the estate in Mochdre in the late 50s and early 60s. He totalled £1,500,000 in transfer fees, and that doesn't happen unless you can play a bit. More than a bit. And yet you can believe it when his old mates tell you he's never changed. Debbie Thomas may have a different story, but then we shouldn't take either side in a sadly broken marriage such as theirs as gospel.

When Mickey came out of prison after serving half of his eighteen-month sentence, he immediately began playing again – for Porthmadog. He can't leave the game alone. The day after that dire Liverpool v Manchester United Cup Final of 1996, Mickey showed them how it should be done. He and Joey Jones turned out for a combined England and Wales side against Rab C. Nesbitt's Scotland XI at Clydebank's Kilbowie Park. They call it playing football with a smile.

The pair of them are a big hit on the Welsh after-dinner circuit now – a ticket to see them at Oswestry Town Supporters Club in 1996 costing a very reasonable £5. Just don't ask him if he's got change for a twenty!

'I've always been a little bit crazy and done my own thing,' says Mickey. 'Don't ask me why, I can't rationalise it myself. I've always acted on a whim depending on my mood, I suppose I just used to get fed up and bugger off. Looking back, I don't know how I got away with it. But I've no regrets, none at all. I've had a long career, plenty of laughs and played for some great clubs. I suppose with the moves I've had I could and should have been a millionaire. But the truth is that money has never been that important to me. I started off with nothing and if I end up with nothing it won't bother me. Mind you, if the police hadn't found my printing machine I'd be as rich as Alan bloody Shearer by now.'

The Welsh George Best. No way! He's the Welsh Mickey Thomas and that should be enough, more than enough, for anyone. Oh, by the way, Mickey, cheers for the bottle of bubbly in Cardiff back in September '85!

MICKEY THOMAS
Born: Mochdre near Colwyn Bay, July 7 1954
5 ft 6 10st 6lbs

Wrexham
April 1972-November 1978 (217 + 13 league 33 goals)

Manchester United
November 1978-August 1981 (90 league apps 11 goals)

Everton
August 1981-November 1981 (10 league apps)

Brighton
November 1981-August 1982 (18 +2 league apps)

Stoke City
August 1982-January 1984 (57 league apps 14 goals)

Chelsea
January 1984-September 1985 (44 league apps 9 goals)

West Bromwich Albion
September 1985-August 1986 (20 league apps)

Derby County on loan – April-May 1986 (9 league apps)

Wichita Wings
August 1986-August 1988 (113 games played by the team)

Shrewsbury Town
August 1988-August 1990 (40 league apps 1 goal)

Leeds United
August 1989-August 1990 (3 league apps)

Stoke City on loan – March-May 1990 (8 league apps)

Stoke City
August 1990-May 1991 (31 + 6 league apps 6 goals)

Wrexham
August 1991-May 1993 (34 league appearances 2 goals)

13: Where Are They Now?

Mickey Thomas

Mickey is still living in the same house in Mochdre, North Wales. Wrexham granted him a testimonial match against Wolverhampton Wanderers in July 1997 and he was hoping to set up his own soccer school for kids in North Wales. He also tours supporters club functions in tandem with Joey Jones as an after-dinner speaking act. The famous locks are no longer in evidence after Mickey took the plunge and had his balding head shaved at the end of the 1996/97 season.

Dave Sexton

The man who took Mickey to Manchester United is still very much involved in the game despite major heart surgery in spring 1997. Sexton is now an established part of the England coaching and scouting staff. He also kept a close eye on Middlesbrough's diminutive Brazilian star, Juninho, visiting him in the north east on several occasions during his time at the club. The Brazilian Mickey Thomas perhaps?

Joey Jones

Joey Jones remains Mickey's best mate. He is currently coach at Wrexham having retired as a player at the age of thirty-seven. He boasts League Championship and European Cup medals from his time at Liverpool and seventy-two Welsh caps.

Alan Ball

Alan Ball left Stoke City shortly before Mickey did in 1983. He went on to manage Portsmouth, Exeter, Southampton and Manchester City before being sacked by the Maine Road outfit.

Brian Flynn

Brian Flynn is the manager at Wrexham as he has been since November 1989. He operates on a shoestring budget but remains determined and cheerful. He places much emphasis on the club's youth policy that has provided not only some great players but also much needed funds with the transfers of Lee Jones and Bryan Hughes.

John Neal

The man who 'discovered' Mickey Thomas and signed him for both Wrexham and Chelsea moved upstairs at Stamford Bridge after the appointment of John Hollins in the summer of 1985. Neal had undergone heart surgery the year before. He has since moved back to live in Wrexham.

Wrexham

The Nationwide League Division Two side narrowly missed out on a play-off spot at the end of the 1996-97 season. They have just moved into a superb new training facility at Gresford.

Wales

The Welsh national team continues to struggle to qualify for, let alone reach, either the European Championship or World Cup. Under manager Bobby Gould the Welsh set-up now has a degree of continuity and stability but this has not been reflected in results and Welsh supporters feel the team is perhaps further away from success now than at any time in living memory. The English FA refused to play Gould's team in a friendly after being approached in 1996 and the Welsh opted instead to play Leyton Orient. Orient won 2-1.

Mochdre

Mochdre remains a quiet village on the road between Colwyn Bay and the dramatic Snowdonian landscape just beyond. The council is engaged in an extensive renovation exercise on the estate where Mickey lives and residents have taken it in turns to live in a collection of mobile homes on the edge of the estate while their own homes are worked on.